This

The graphics of Japanese Confection

Wagashi

Kazuya Takaoka
Mutsuo Takahashi
Hiroshi Yoda

Wagashi

Book and cover design © 2003 Kazuya Takaoka
Selection and Text copyright © 2003 Mutsuo Takahashi
Photographs copyright © 2003 Hiroshi Yoda
English Text copyright © 2003 Emiko Miyashita & Lee Gurga
Published by PIE BOOKS

PIE BOOKS
2-32-4, Minami-Otsuka, Toshima-ku, Tokyo 170-0005 Japan
Tel: +81-3-5395-4811 Fax: +81-3-5395-4812
http://www.piebooks.com
e-mail: editor@piebooks.com e-mail: sales@piebooks.com

ISBN 4-89444-288-4 C0072
Printed in Japan

和の菓子

高岡一弥

高橋睦郎

与田弘志

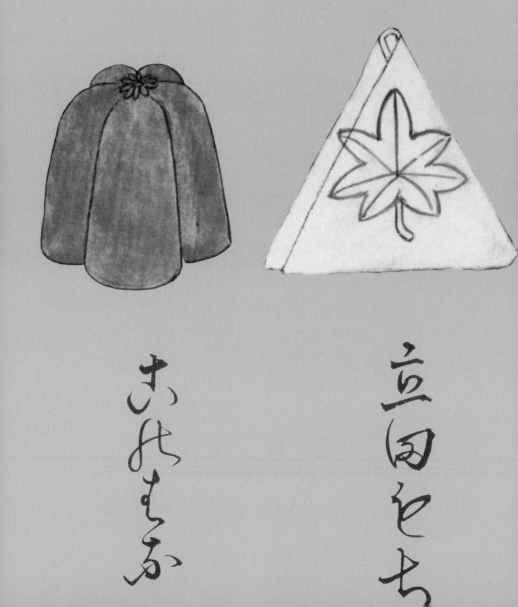

さ
れ
も
か

立
同
セ
ち

茶の一碗すなはちさし出し

A bowl of tea thus held out,

小やかの菓子すなはち勧む

A small sweet thus offered,

客はこれ一の旅神

The guest is a god on a journey.

座はこれ去来の間

His seat lies between past and future.

失名氏　Anonymous

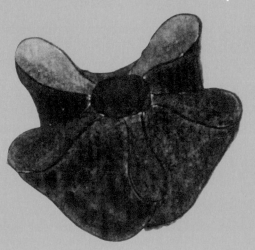

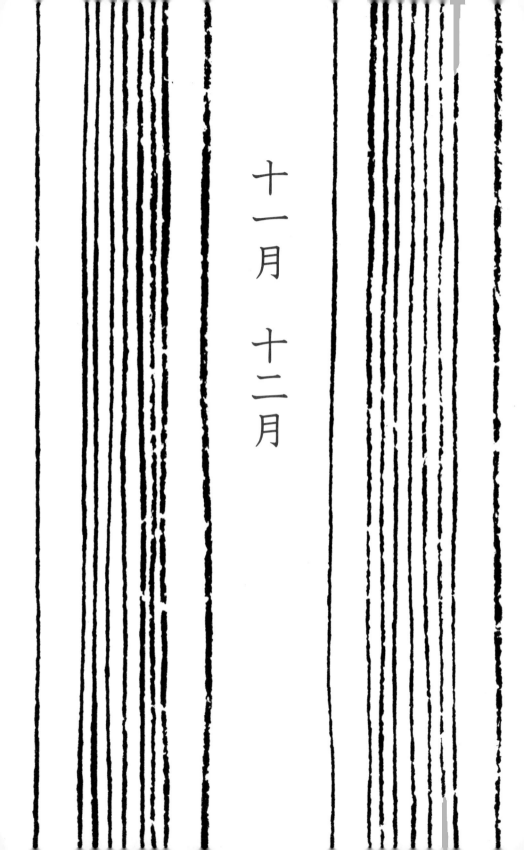

十一月　十二月

November

December

In the calendar, early November is the time that shifts from autumn to winter, yet the weather often remains comparatively mild and warm. *Irori,* the hearth sunk into the floor in the farmer's house and *kotatsu,* an enclosed hearth with a coverlet, in the tradesman's house are brought into use. The opening day of the sunken hearth, which can be regarded as the New Year's Day for the tea ceremony, is also held at this time of the year. The calendar of Japanese confections starts its year according to this tradition, too. December, which follows, is the month in which one completes the whole year by tidying things up in the household, carrying out a general house cleaning, and preparing for the coming New Year. In the hills and fields, we can see the remaining tint on the grasses and tree leaves; birds are busy pecking at their last sustenance. In the northern areas, the snow starts to fall and ice begins to form at the water's edge.

暦の上では十一月初旬に秋が終わり冬に入るが、比較的あたたかい、おだやかな日がつづく。農家の囲炉裏、町家の炬燵もこの頃から使われた。お茶の世界の正月といえる炉開きもこの時期。日本の菓子の暦もこれに従う。つづく十二月は一年をしめくくって家内を片づけ大掃除をし、新しい年を迎える年用意をする月。野山には草木が紅葉を残し、小鳥たちが最後の餌を求めていそがしい。北の地方では雪が降りはじめ、水辺が氷を結びはじめる。

鳥不宿

Tatsuta Cake

Tatsutamochi, November
Tatsuta in Yamato Province is renowned
for its tinted maple leaves.
The autumn goddess Princess Tatsuta
was named after this place.
On a pale pink skin wrapping *koshian*,
strained bean jam, is a brand mark of a maple leaf.
A refined confection typical of late autumn.
Kawabatadōki

龍田餅　十一月
大和国龍田は紅葉の名所、
龍田の地名に因む龍田姫は秋の女神。
こし餡を包んだ淡紅色の皮に紅葉の焼印
晩秋・初冬のゆかしい菓子だ。
川端道喜

たつたもち

はかまごしもち

袴腰餅　十二月
その昔　宮中では年末の吉日を選んで
女官たちが御煤払いをおこない、
済んで御献があり　菓子を賜わった。
その日の女官たちの袴姿を象っている。

川端道喜

Hakamagoshimochi,　December
In olden times, in the Imperial Court,
an auspicious day was chosen at the end of the year
for the minor court ladies to sweep it clean of soot.
Afterwards there was *gokon*, the serving of rice wine,
and each was given a confection.
This cake depicts the minor court lady
in her pleated skirt on that day.
Kawabatadōki

Pleated Skirt Cake

Shaded Tinted Leaves

Shitamomiji, November
Ancient people did not miss the beauty of the
colored leaves in the shade while appreciating the
bright ones on the sunny side.
The difference in color and shade between the
upper and lower leaves truly embodies the name
momiji no nishiki, brocade of tinted leaves.
Kameyaiori

下紅葉　十一月
古人は日の当たる上葉の紅葉だけではなく
日当り乏しい下葉の紅葉も見のがさなかった。
下葉と上葉の色彩の変化階調によって
紅葉の錦は　錦の名にふさわしくなる。
亀屋伊織

したもみじ

Gingko Rice Cracker

Ichō senbei, November
For *momiji*, tinted leaves, we have two sets of *kanji*
or Chinese characters; one is red leaves,
and the other is yellow leaves.
If the typical red leaf is a maple's,
the typical yellow leaf would be the gingko's.
A brand of a gingko leaf is marked in the
middle of a *tanesenbei*, rice cracker.
Kameyaiori

銀杏煎餅　十一月
モミジには紅葉と黄葉の字を当てる。
紅いモミジの代表がカエデモミジなら
黄色いモミジの代表はイチョウモミジ。
種煎餅にイチョウの焼印を押した。
亀屋伊織

いちょうせんべい

にしきだい、もみじせんべい

錦台、紅葉煎餅　十一月
カエデの語源はカエルデ、蛙の手。
青楓がアオガエルの手なら
楓紅葉はアカガエルの手か。

どのカエルも冬眠に入る季節だ。

亀屋伊織

Nishikidai Momiji Senbei,　November
The etymology of *kaede*, maple, is *kaerude*, frog's hands. If *aokaede*,
green maple leaves, were the hands of *aogaeru*, green frogs,
then would *kaede momiji*, colored maple leaves,
be the hands of *akagaeru*, red frogs?
This is the time of the year when all the frogs
begin their hibernation.
Kameyaiori

Hill of Brocade　Colored Leaf Rice Cracker

Wind-driven Leaves

Fukiyose, November

Fukiyose, wind-driven leaves,
consists of seven varieties of confections: *kuri*,
chestnut, *matsukasa*, pine cone, *ginnan*, gingko nuts,
kinoko, mushroom, *ichō*, gingko leaf, *matsuba*,
pine needle, and *momiji*, tinted maple leaf.
When these are served together in a dish,
one can see why they were given the name of *fukiyose*.
They appear exactly as if they had been driven
into the dish by the early winter wind.
This group of seven confections was first thought
to have been brought together to make use of the
leftovers from the previous day's sale.
Kameyaiori

吹きよせ　十一月
クリ、マツカサ、ギンナン、キノコ、
イチョウ、マツバ、モミジの七種。
文字通り　初冬の風が吹き寄せた風情。
もとは売れ残りを集めた始末の知恵から。
亀屋伊織

ふきよせ

まつば

松葉　十一月

冬になっても翠（みどり）みずみずしいマツは
常葉木（ときわぎ）の代表として、古来大切にされる。
常葉木－西洋流にいうなら　永遠の樹、
宇宙樹ということになろうか。

亀屋伊織

Matsuba, November
Since ancient times, *matsu,* pine trees,
with their fresh green *matsuba,* needles,
have been highly esteemed as the representative *tokiwagi,*
trees with eternally green leaves.
Perhaps in Western culture we might
be able to use expressions like
"eternal tree" or "cosmic tree"
to explain the word combining *tokiwa,*
the rock that never changes, with *gi,* tree.
Kameyaiori

Pine Needles

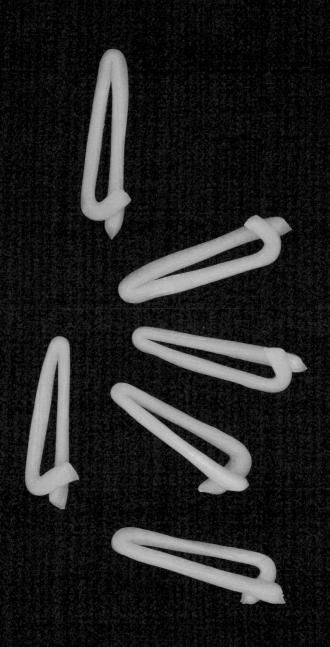

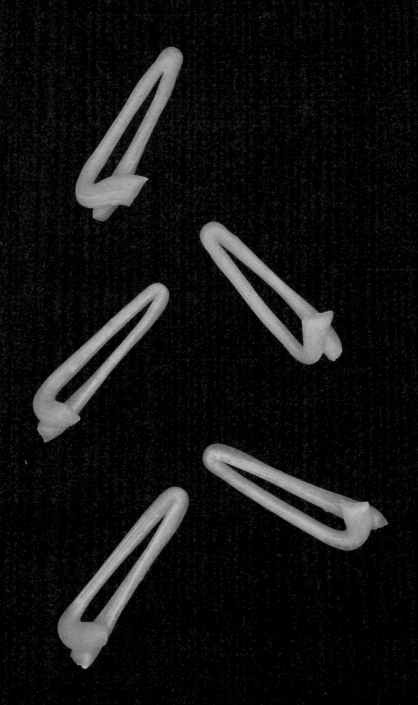

Withered Pine Needles

Karematsuba, November

Pine trees, which are classified as evergreen conifers,
nevertheless do drop their needles.
In fact, if we take a close look at the trees,
the budding of new leaves
can be seen at a certain time of the year.
Tea masters save the fallen pine needles
and enjoy the beauty of *shikimatsuba*,
scattered pine needles, in their gardens.
Kameyaiori

枯松葉　十一月
常緑針葉樹といわれるマツも　よく見れば
古葉が落ち新葉が育つ新陳代謝が。
茶人たちは　古葉を捨てず庭に敷く、
いわゆる敷松葉の風情を愉しんで来た。
亀屋伊織

かれまつば

Snow Ring

Yukiwa, December
Long before the invention of the microscope,
ancient people had known
that crystals of snow are hexagonal.
While preserving the snowflake's hexagonal shape,
some appear more round.
A shape born of the sense of
traditionel Japanese beauty.
Kameyaiori

雪輪　十二月
顕微鏡など存在しない昔から　古人は
雪の結晶が六角形であることを知っていた。
その六角形をそのままに　さらに円形に。
日本人の伝統的美意識の生んだかたちだ。
亀屋伊織

Kōrin's Pine

Kōrinmatsu, December
Kōrin Ogata was a painter in Kyoto
in the middle of the Edo Period who established
his own bold and gorgeous style of decorative painting.
The patterns and designs he created
are called *Kōrin moyō*, Kōrin's designs.
Kōrin matsu, Kōrin's pine, is one of his masterpieces.
Kameyaiori

光琳松　十二月
江戸中期の京都の絵師　尾形光琳は
大胆・華麗な装飾画の大成者。
彼の考案した模様は光琳模様と呼ばれる。
光琳松も光琳模様の傑作の一つ。
亀屋伊織

こうりんまつ

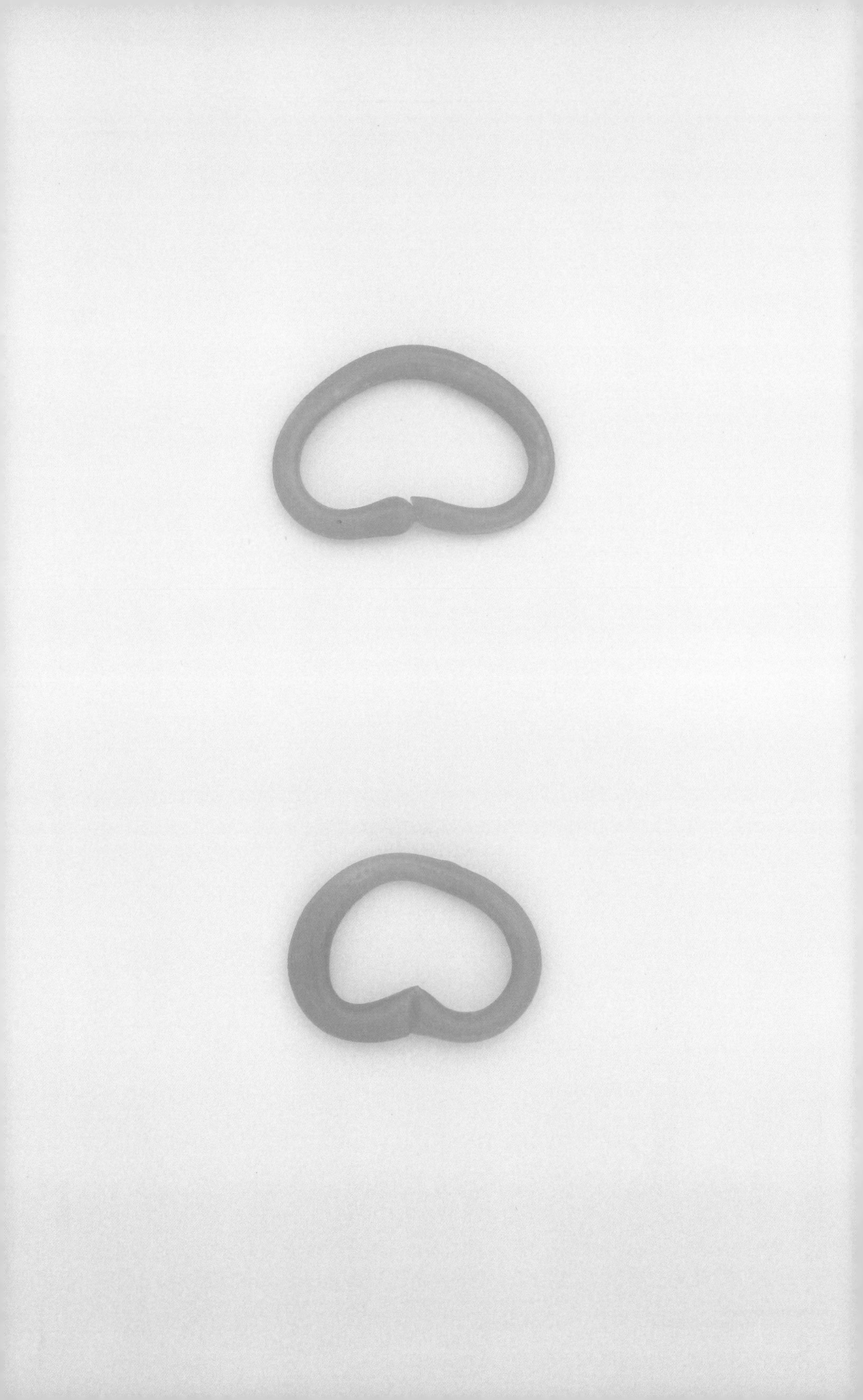

Brocade of the Mountain Path

Yamaji no nishiki, November

The colored leaves of late autumn and early winter differ
from tree to tree; for this reason they have been compared
to brocade imported from China.
The cinnamon-flavored bean jam is the
distinctive ingredient of this sweet.

Toraya

山路の錦　十一月

晩秋・初冬の木々の紅葉は
木の種類ごとに色とりどり、
昔から　中国渡りの錦に喩えられる。
肉桂入りの御膳餡に特徴がある。
とらや

やまじのにしき

もみじやき

紅葉焼　十一月
林間に紅葉を焼き　酒を暖めるとは
中国唐の詩人のなつかしい詩句。
饅頭の白い肌に押された紅葉の焼印、
その上の仄かな紅が火を思わせる。
とらや

Momijiyaki, November
Making a bonfire in the woods with tinted leaves
to warm the wine is a phrase from a charming poem written
by a poet in Tang dynasty China.
The brand mark of tinted leaves is
pressed on the top of the white bun,
its faint crimson reminds of fire.
Toraya

Bonfire of Tinted Leaves

まんせんまき

万千巻　十一月
万も　千も　長寿や祝賀を意味する数。
黄　紅　白の三色の生地が渦を巻く形に。
慶びや幸いが幾久しくつづくようにとの
願いがこめられているようだ。
とらや

Mansenmaki, November
Both a thousand and ten thousand are numbers
used to indicate longevity and celebration.
A prayer for long-lasting happiness
and good fortune can be sensed in the whirl of yellow,
red, and white dough.
Toraya

A Thousand and Ten Thousand Roll

Layered Tinted Leaves

Momijigasane, November
There are *kōyō*, red leaves, and *kōyō*, yellow leaves,
among *momiji*, tinted leaves.
The beauty of the hills and fields is highlighted
by the combination of the two.
Kasane, layering, is also written as '襲', *kasane*.
The word *kasane* also refers to the beauty resulting
from the combination of two colors according
to the sense of beauty current during the Heian Period.
Toraya

紅葉重ね　十一月
モミジには紅葉と黄葉があり
その色の階調が秋の野山を美しくする。
重ねは襲ねとも書き　平安時代の美意識が生んだ
二つの色の取り合わせの映り合いをもいう。
とらや

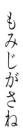

もみじがさね

Awaji Lagoon

Awajigata, November
The first island created together
by the mythical figures Iazanagi and
Izanami was called Awajishima.
The plovers are chirping
and flying over the mud flats.
This has long been a subject for many *tanka* poetry.
Toraya

淡路潟　十一月
神話のイザナギ・イザナミが
最初に産んだ島が淡路島。
初冬の干潟には千鳥が鳴き渡り
多くの歌に詠まれて来た。
とらや

あ
わ
じ
が
た

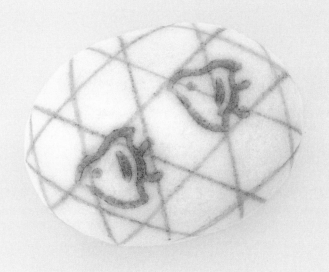

Quail Rice Cake

Uzuramochi, November

Uzura, quail, belongs to the pheasant family,
but has a rounder body and shorter tail than a pheasant.
It walks around the autumn grass fields crying
in a piercing voice.
The figure of the quail has been cherished
by many *waka* poets; the shape is
simplified here and made into a *mochigashi,*
a rice cake.

Toraya

鶉餅　十一月

ウズラはキジの仲間だが　丸々して尾が短く
秋の草原を這いまわって　鋭く鳴く。
歌人たちに愛されてきたその姿を
単純化して　餅菓子にした。
とらや

うずらもち

Mandarin Orange Cake

Mikanmochi, November

In ancient times, the mandarin orange was
called *tokijikunokagunokonomi,*
the year-round fragrant fruit.
Tajimamori was said to have brought it
from the Land of the Eternity.
White bean jam mixed with thick malt syrup
is wrapped in starch paste and is formed
into the shape of a mandarin orange.
Toraya

蜜柑餅　十一月
ミカンは古く非時香菓（ときじくのかぐのこのみ）と呼ばれ
田道間守（たじまもり）が常世国（とこよのくに）からもたらしたという。
水飴を加え練りあげた白餡を求肥（ぎゅうひ）で包み
ミカンのかたちを象っている。
とらや

みかんもち

Winter Hibernation

Fuyugomori, December

Winter confinement refers to a state
in which living things are enduring the long winter,
waiting patiently for spring.
The strength of life in the cold is expressed by the
red steamed bean paste.
the falling snow by the yam flakes.

Toraya

冬籠　十二月
冬ごもりとは　もののいのちが
長い冬に耐えて春を待ちつづけること。
寒さの中の生命の強さを紅色の羊羹製で
降りつむ雪を山芋のそぼろで表現している。
とらや

ふゆごもり

こおりのうえ

氷の上　十二月
スイセンは冬を代表する吉祥の花。
雪の中に咲くことから雪中花とも呼ばれる。
寒い冬、氷りついた水辺近くに咲く
スイセンの端正な姿を表現している。
とらや

Kōrinoue, December
Narcissus is a typical winter flower that is considered an auspicious sign.
It is also called mid-snow-flower for it blooms in the snow.
In the cold winter weather, it blooms near the icy shores.
This confection represents the classical features of the narcissus.
Toraya

On the Ice

まつがさね

松襲　十二月
襲は平安朝の美意識が生んだ
色の組み合わせのこと。
緑が冬も色変えぬマツの葉のめでたさを
紫がその影を表わす　という。
とらや

Matsugasane, December
Kasane is the layering of two colors.
It is born of the sense of beauty of the *Heian* Period.
Green is said to represent the propitious sign
of the pine needles
which do not change their color
in winter, and purple their shadows.
Toraya

Layered Colors of Pine

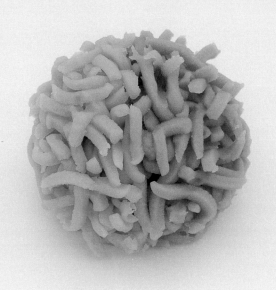

らくようのみち

洛陽のみち　十二月
洛陽は漢の都　比喩的に京都を指す。
京都の道路は碁盤の目状で知られる。
平成十五年の宮中歌会始のお題
「町」に因んで考案された。
とらや

Rakuyō no michi, December
Rakuyō was the capital of Han in China;
the name also came to be used to refer Kyoto,
the Imperial capital of Japan.
Kyoto is known for its neat grid of streets.
This confection was devised from the subject,
"town", at the Imperial Court's New Year Poetry
Party in the fifteenth year of the Heisei Era (2003).
Toraya

Streets of Rakuyo

Yuzu Citron Shape

Yugata, December

Yuzu citron is a representative fragrance
of late autumn and early winter.
Sour juice is squeezed from it and used in many dishes,
such as *yuzu gama, yuzu miso*, etc.
The *yuzu* bath on the night of winter solstice is well known.
This is a variation of *mikanmochi*,
Mandarin orange cake.
Toraya

柚形　十二月
晩秋・初冬の香りを代表するのがユズ。
搾って酢にし、柚釜　柚味噌等　用途は広い。
冬至の柚子湯もよく知られている。
蜜柑餅のヴァリエーション。
とらや

ゆがた

Beach Plover

Hamachidori, December
Chidori, plovers,
are aquatic birds living in the marshes of a bay,
or in lakes and ponds.
Those who live primarily
at the seaside are called *hamachidori*,
beach plovers, or *urachidori*, bay plovers.
They make footprints on the beach
sand and sing while they are flying.
The confection represents the bird's footprints
on the sand.
Toraya

浜千鳥　十二月
チドリは江湾の干潟や湖沼に住む水辺の鳥。
とくに海辺にいるものを　浜千鳥、浦千鳥などと呼ぶ。
沙の上に足跡をつけて　鳴きながら飛ぶ。
菓子は沙上につけた鳥跡を表わす。
とらや

はまちどり

Mount Fuji in Four Seasons Winter

Shiki no fuji Fuyu, December

Needless to say, Mount Fuji is the symbol of Japan.
The snow covering its peak is expressed by the *dōmyōjikan,*
jelly of ground glatinous rice powder,
which emphasizes the purity of winter.

Toraya

四季の富士　冬　十二月

富士山はいうまでもなく日本の象徴
その上に降る雪を道明寺羹で表わし
冬季の清浄感を強調した。
とらや

しきのふじ　ふゆ

一月、二月

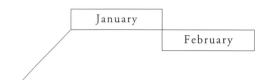

January

February

Since the opening of our country in the Meiji Era, the shift from the Chinese lunar calendar to the solar calendar has caused some divergence in our sense of the seasons. The New Year in the Chinese lunar calendar is about six weeks later than that in the solar calendar; thus the New Year is more closely associated with the beginning of spring than with the middle of winter as it is in the solar calendar. With the arrival of the solar New Year, we still maintain the imminence of spring. In the Imperial Court, at the *Outakaihajime*, New Year Poetry Party, the recitation begins with the New Year's *tanka* poems composed by the Emperor and Empress. Noh begins its year with a performance of *Okina*, "An Aged Man", which celebrates spring. The program in the Kabuki Theater is titled, *Hatsuharu Kyōgen*, "The Early Spring Noh Farce". On January seventh, the seven kinds of spring herbs are picked to cook *nanakusagayu*, the porridge of seven herbs; on February third which is *Setsubun*, the day before the first day of spring, roasted soybeans are made to perform *oniyarai*, the bashing of demons. Such customs, and others, are still active. In tea ceremony, *hatsugama*, first tea ceremony, and *yobanashi* no *chaji*, tea ceremony held on a winter evening, are performed. Also among the variety of confections in this season, we can find many refined ones that are related to the New Year and the arrival of the new spring.

明治開国このかた、太陰暦が太陽暦に変わり、季節感に多少のずれが生じたとはいえ、新年に新しい春を感じる気分は持続した。宮中では御歌会始で天皇・皇后以下の新春の歌が詠みあげられ、能は春を寿ぐ翁から始まり、歌舞伎は初春狂言と銘打たれる。一月七日に春の七草を摘んで七草粥を炊き、二月三日の節分に大豆を煎って鬼やらいをする習慣も健在だ。お茶は初釜に夜咄の茶事、菓子にも新年・新春に因んだゆかしいものがたくさんある。

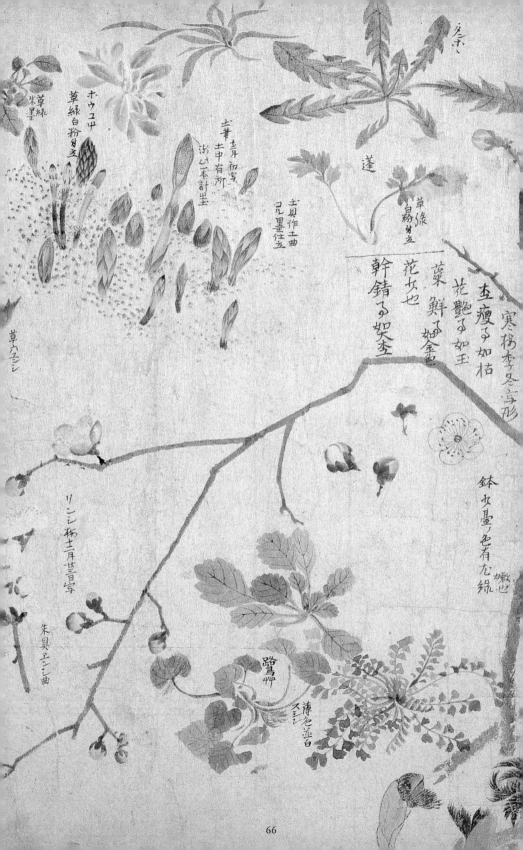

Flower Petal Cake

Hishihanabiramochi, January

Two thin layers of pink and white *mochi,*
rice cake, are folded in half; inside are *misoan,*
soybean paste flavored bean jam, and *fukusagobō,*
the sticks of sweet boiled burdock imitating *oshiayu,*
a salted sweet fish, characteristic of the New Year's dish
in the Imperial Court.
A typical confection associated
with the New Year's functions at the Imperial Court.

Kawabatadōki

菱葩餅　一月
薄く伸ばした紅白の餅を重ね、
押鮎見立ての袱紗牛蒡を置き、
二つ折りに　味噌餡をくるみ込む。
宮中正月行事に因む雅びの典型の菓子。
川端道喜

ひしはなびらもち

Midwinter Crimson Plum Blossom

Kankōbai, February
Michizane Sugawara, who was called Kankō
out of respect, died in disgrace after being removed
from the position of the Minister of the Right
as a result of being slandered.
He is viewed with much sympathy by the Japanese.
He was also a refined poet who loved plum blossoms.
In February, the Plum Blossom Festival
is held in memory of his tragedy.

Kawabatadōki

寒紅梅　二月
左大臣の身分から　讒言で左遷され
配所に没した菅公は　日本人好みのヒーロー。
彼はまた梅花を愛する風流の詩人でもあった。
二月にはその悲劇を偲ぶ梅花祭が催される。
川端道喜

かんこうばい

うめごろも

梅衣　二月
「ウメの香りは白にあって、紅になく、
淡紅梅には仄かにある」という。
淡紅梅色の薄く延ばした餅皮に餡を包み、
梅花の印を押した品位ある菓子だ。
川端道喜

Umegoromo, February
It is said that the fragrance of plum blossoms
stays in the white ones but not in the crimson ones,
and is only faintly present in the pale pink ones.
The cake is coated with a pale pink plum blossom colored
mochi with bean jam inside,
and a plum blossom stamp is pressed on top.
A very elegant sweet.
Kawabatadōki

Plum Blossom Robe

つばきもち

椿餅　二月
ツバキはウメとともに春の魁の花、
その常緑の葉二枚で挟んだ餅菓子。
『源氏物語』には「つばいもちひ」の名で登場。
最古の歴史を持つ和菓子の一つ。
川端道喜

Tsubakimochi,　February
Camellia, along with plum blossoms,
is a harbinger of the spring season.
The cake is layered between two evergreen leaves of camellia.
It appears in *The Tale of Genji*
where it is called *tsubaimochihi*.
One of the confections with
the oldest history.
Kawabatadōki

Camellia Cake

Plum Blossom Rice Cracker

Ume senbei, February
Introduced from ancient China,
plum trees have taught the Japanese the joy
of appreciating their blossoms.
Bean jam is placed between the
two pale plum-blossom colored *tanesenbei*,
rice crackers with a mark in the middle.
The mark is a plum blossom.
A simple yet refined confectionery.
Kameyaiori

梅煎餅　二月
古代中国から舶来して　日本人に
花を愛でることを教えてくれたウメ。
淡紅梅色の種煎餅二枚に餡をはさみ、
梅の焼印を押しただけのゆかしい干菓子。
亀屋伊織

うめせんべい

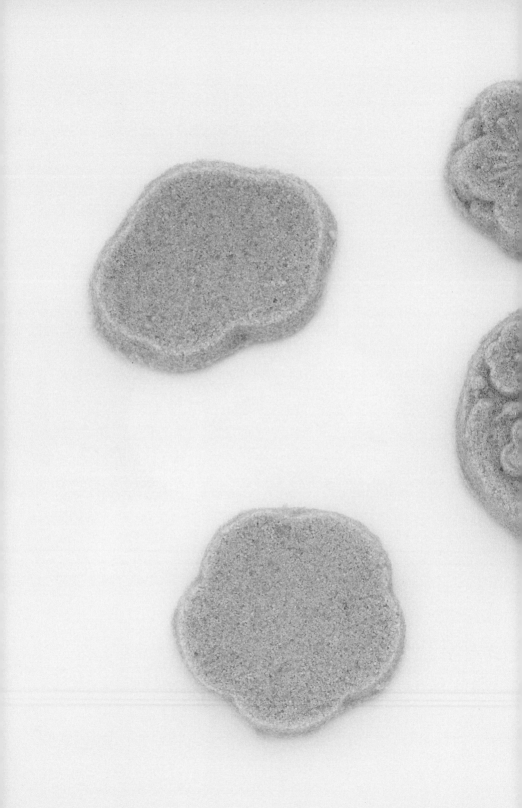

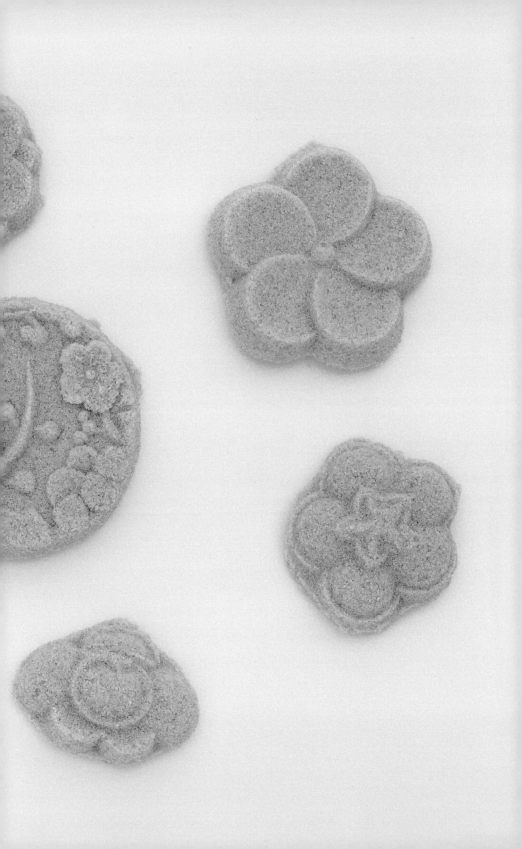

う
め

梅　二月
ウメは中国四川省あたりが原産地。
これを受け入れた上代のわが国では
男性は白梅を　女性は紅梅を好んだ。
男性は香りを　女性は色を好んだわけだ。
亀屋伊織

Ume, February
Ume, the plum tree, originates in China's Szechwan province.
When it was brought to Japan in the Nara Period,
the white plum blossoms were preferred
by men and the crimson blossoms were favored by women.
The men preferred the fragrance and the
women appreciated the color.
Kameyaiori

Plum

Twisted Bar

Nejiribō, February

Red and white toffee are twisted like Japanese
reins and then shaped into a bar.
It may also be modeled after a cord
hanging from the huge bell in front of a shrine;
those praying pull it to ring the bell
on occasions like *Setsubun*,
the day before the first day of spring,
and *Hatsuuma*,
the Inari shrine festival held on the
first day of the Horse in February.
Kameyaiori

ねじりぼう　二月
紅白の有平糖を手綱様にねじり
棒状に仕上げたもの。
節分・初午の神前で手に持って鳴らす
大鈴の鈴の緒を象ったものだろうか。
亀屋伊織

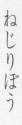

きつねめん

きつね面　二月
二月はお稲荷さんの初午祭の月。
お稲荷さんの眷族(けんぞく)はキツネ。
境内の子供たちのお面をヒントにした
亀屋伊織先代の飄逸な傑作。
亀屋伊織

Kitsunemen, February
February is the month for the
Hatsuuma Festival of the Inari Shrine.
The followers of the gods and goddesses
enshrined in the Inari Shrine are foxes.
A buoyant masterpiece made by the
late proprietor of Kameya Iori,
it gives a hint of the fox masks
children wear at the shrine's fair.
Kameyaiori

Fox Mask

Favoring Studies Blossom

Kōbunka, January

When Wu-di of the state of Jin in ancient China was studying,
the blossoms of the plum tree opened,
but when he neglected his studies they closed.
Kōbunboku, favoring-studies tree,
was the name given to the plum tree from this legend.
Kanshōjō, Minster of the Right, Michizune Sugawara,
was also known to favor the plum blossoms.

Toraya

好文花　一月
中国晋の武帝が学問に励むと花ひらき
怠ると花を閉じたという故事から
ウメの木の別名を「好文木」という。
さてこそ　菅丞相も梅を好んだ。
とらや

こうぶんか

88

Camellia Cake

Tsubakimochi, January

The ancient Japanese people particularly prized camellias;
what they valued were the leaves rather than the blossoms.
We can assume that this resulted from the belief
that divine spirits descended on the evergreen trees
which remain unchanged throughout the four seasons.

Toraya

椿餅　一月
古代日本人は　ことさらツバキを
それも花よりも葉を大切にした。
四季を通じて常緑の木には　神霊が
降りてくるという信仰のせいらしい。
とらや

つばきもち

はなごろも

花衣　一月
花はサクラというのは　平安時代以降のこと、
それ以前は　花といえばウメのことだった。
紅梅色の三角形の羊羹製に小倉餡を乗せ
三方から包み込み　梅の押印を配す。
とらや

Hanagoromo, January
Hana, "the blossoms" means cherry blossoms,
but this became so only after the Heian Period;
before that "blossoms" meant plum blossoms.
Oguraan, bean jam mixed with cooked beans,
is placed on a red plum colored triangular *mushi-yōkan*,
steamed bean paste, and wrapped from three sides,
a plam mark is pressed on each side.
Toraya

Plum Blossom Robe

はるどなり

春隣　一月
春隣とは春がもうそこまで来ている気分をいう
平安時代このかたの由緒正しい晩冬の季詞。
茶色のそぼろの上に黄色のそぼろを置き
土から顔を出したフクジュソウを表現。
とらや

Harudonari, January
Harudonari, spring in the neighborhood,
captures a feeling of approaching spring.
Since the Heain Period it has been a time-
honored *ki no kotoba*,
seasonal word, expressing a warm spell in late winter.
On top of brown *soboro*,
intricate bits of bean paste,
yellow *soboro* is placed,
depicting the appearance of *fukujusō*
(happy and long life grass),
adonis, from under the soil.
Toraya

Spring in the Neighborhood   94

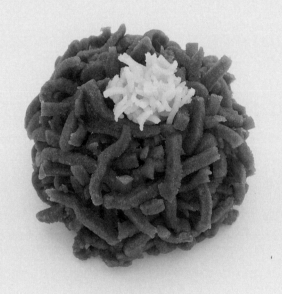

Smiling Face Cake

Egaoman, January
Among the New Year's *kidai*, seasonal expressions,
are *hatsuwarai*, the first laughter of the year,
and *fukuwarai*, happy laughter.
The happy year begins with the happy laughter
on New Year's Day.
On the pure white *jōyomanjū* a tiny red dot is placed
to represent a smiling face in the wish
for it to become the starting point of one's happy New Year.
Toraya

笑顔饅　一月
新年に初笑い　福笑いの季題があるが
倖せな一年は　元旦の笑顔から。
薯蕷饅頭の純白の肌に一点の紅を置いて
倖せな一年の原点となる笑顔を表わした。
とらや

え
が
お
ま
ん

ちょうせいもち

長生餅　一月
正月初子（はつね）の日、松苗を根ごと引く小松引きは
根の長さにあやかり、長生を願う占い習俗。
薯蕷饅頭（じょうよまんじゅう）の白い肌には根引松（ねびきまつ）の焼印を押しただけ。
新年にふさわしい、めでたい菓子だ。
とらや

Chōseimochi, January

On the first occurrence of the Rat's Day in the New Year,

in a wish for longevity a pine sapling

is pulled out to augur by the length of its roots.

A mark representing this pine is simple against the

white skin of *jōyomanjū*,

a steamed bun of yam and rice-powder skin

with bean jam inside.

An auspicious cake,

appropriate for celebrating the New Year.

Toraya

Long Life Cake

このはなぶんこ

木の花文庫　二月
わが国最初の勅撰和歌集「古今集」には
仮名序に「灘波津に咲くや木花」の歌が登場。
歌にいう「木花」とはウメのこと。
饅頭を梅模様の手文庫に見立てた。
とらや

Konohana bunko, February
In the introduction of *Kokinwakashū*,
the first national anthology of *tanka* poetry in Japan,
a poem which begins with the phrase,
"*Naniwazu ni sakuya konohana*",
'Blossoming in Naniwazu Bay are *konohana*',appears.
Konohana in *tanka* poetry is the plum blossom.
The cake is likened to a plum-patterned box
for keeping letters and stationery.
Toraya

Plum Blossom Patterned Box

はるのやま

春の山　二月
春の訪れを待ちわびて　山にのぼり
若草を包むのは　山里の子等の愉しみ。
白い薯蕷饅頭にさわらびの焼印を押し
さみどりを配した早春の菓子。
とらや

Harunoyama, February
After longing for the arrival of spring,
it is a great joy to climb a mountain to pick the fresh
herbs for the children living in the mountain country.
On the top of a white *jōyomanjū*,
a yam bun stuffed with bean jam,
a brand mark of fresh bracken contrasts
with a touch of herbs' fresh green.
An early spring confection.
Toraya

Spring Mountain

Oribe's Cake

Oribeman, February

Oribeyaki is a kind of pottery created by Oribe Furuta.
Its characteristic is the bold contrast of green and brown.
The pattern of the brand mark reminds us of the
departing winter; the gradated green implies the
approaching spring.

Toraya

織部饅　二月
茶人古田織部の考案という織部焼は
緑色と茶色の大胆なコントラストが一つの特徴。
焼印の模様が去りゆく冬を
ぼかしの緑が訪れる春を連想させる。
とらや

Midwinter Crimson Plum Blossom

Kankōbai, February

When the word *hana*, blossom, is mentioned alone,
it refers specifically to cherry blossoms.
Plum blossoms are referred to as *hana no ani*,
the elder brothers of cherry blossoms.
Guided by the elder brother of blossoms we,
the Japanese, have leaned to appreciate *hana*,
cherry blossoms.
Toraya

寒紅梅　二月

ただ花とだけいえば、サクラのこと。
ウメのことは花に対して花の兄という。
花の兄－ウメに導かれて、日本人は
花－サクラを愛でることを覚えた。
とらや

かんこうばい

みちとせ

三千歳　二月
不老長生を願う漢の武帝のもとに
三千年に一度実る仙桃がもたらされた。
西方を支配する女神西王母の贈物という。
伝統に因んで　モモの花を象っている。
とらや

Michitose, February
Wu-Di of Former Han Dynasty,
who wished for perennial youth and immortality,
was given a fruit of the *sentō*
or wizard's peach by Seiōbo,
a goddess ruling the western region. According to legend,
the wizard's peach ripens only once every three thousand years.
The cake is thus shaped like a peach blossom.
Toraya

Three Thousand Years

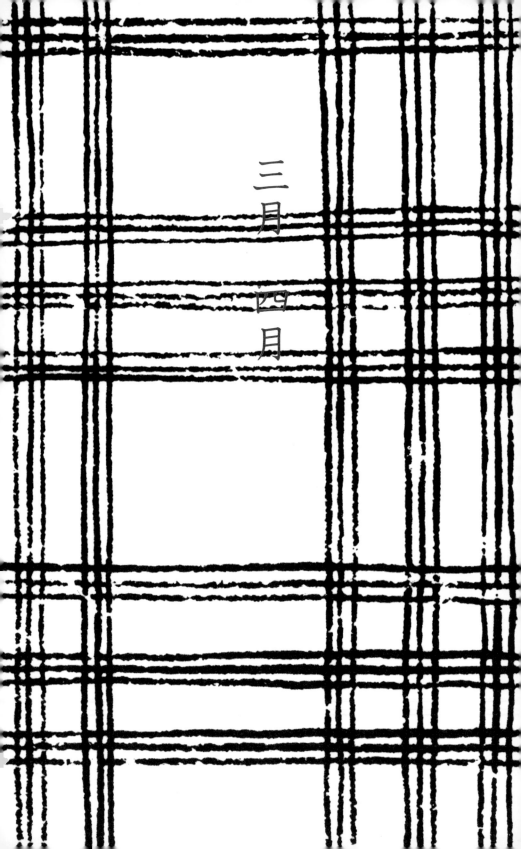

三月

四月

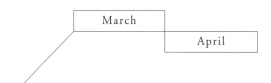

March

April

March third is the Doll's Festival Day during which *hinaningyō*, the Festival dolls, are displayed on red-carpeted tiered platforms. Girls drink *shirozake*, a sweet drink made from fermented rice, and eat *hinagashi*, Doll Festival sweets. In the middle of the month, *Otaimatsu*, the Bamboo Flambeau ceremony, and *Omizutori*, the Water-drawing ceremony, are held in Tōdaiji Temple in Nara. The Buddhist memorial services are performed during *Ohigan,* the equinoctial week. For the rest of the month reports of the opening of the cherry blossoms are heard one by one starting from the southern region of the country. By the time April arrives, the entire country is tinted in one color, that of the cherry blossoms. People vacillate between hope and despair at the change of weather which can quicken the opening of the blossoms and also make them fall. They visit and enjoy the famous cherry blossom-viewing spots around the country. Many confections of the season are given flowery names and flavors related to cherry blossoms.

三月三日は雛祭、赤い毛氈を敷いた雛壇に雛人形を飾り、少女たちが白酒を飲み、雛菓子を食べる。中旬は奈良東大寺のおたいまつ、お水取り。下旬に入りお彼岸を過ぎると、南から順に各地の花便りが聞かれはじめる。そして、四月になれば日本じゅうが花一色、桜一色に覆われる。

人々は桜花を開かせ、桜花を散らす天気の変化に一喜一憂し、そちこちの桜の名所に繰り出して、花見を愉しむ。菓子にも桜に因む華やかな名と味を持つものが多い。

鬼嫩綠
同点
莢赤也

ヲシ墨
ミ茇臭炎
少孫加甘立

狗脊

草茶ヲシ甘立

114

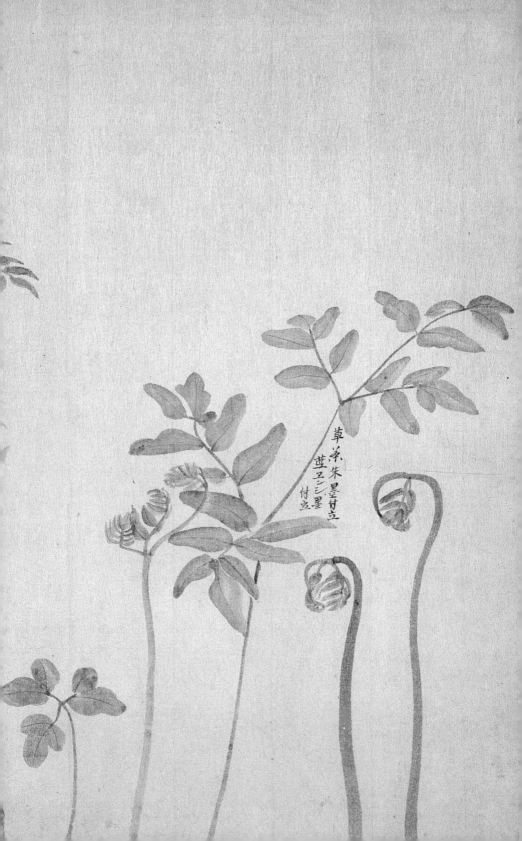

草茎朱
墨付立
並ヱ二ハ墨
付立

Young Grass

Wakakusa, March

Bean jam is wrapped in *dōmyōjikawa*,
a skin made of ground glutinous rice powder,
tinted the color of young grass.
It is covered with plenty of powdered *kōrimochi*,
freeze-dried rice cake.
This cake reminds us of life sprouting from under the snow.
An elegant confection suitable for the early spring.

Kawabatadōki

若草　三月
道明寺皮を若草色に染めて、餡を包み
氷餅の粉をたっぷりつけた仕上げ。
雪の下から萌え出るいのちを思わせる
早春にふさわしい格調高い餅菓子。

川端道喜

さ
が
の
は
る

嵯峨の春　四月
春秋に天皇の行幸が相次いだ嵯峨野。
ことに春は嵐山や大沢のサクラで知られる。
淡紅の道明寺皮にふられた氷餅の粉は
桜花を雪に喩えた古歌を思い出させる。
川端道喜

Saga no haru, April
The Emperors used to make visits to Sagano in spring and autumn.
In spring, Arashiyama and Ōsawa in Sagano
are especially known for their cherry blossoms.
The powdered *kōrimochi* sprinkled over the pale pink *dōmyōjikawa*
reminds us of the classical *tanka* poems which
compared cherry blossoms with snow.
Kawabatadōki

Spring in Sagano

Cherry Petal Raft

Hanaikada, April
Hanaikada is a name given to a mass of fallen
cherry petals floating on a stream,
 comparing it with a raft made of wood.
When served, several cakes are usually arranged
in a bowl to form the shape of a raft.
A confection suitable for minds lamenting
the departure of the spring.
Kawabatadōki

花筏　四月
散ったサクラの葩が群れ流れるさまを
木を組んで流す筏に喩えて、花筏という。
鉢に盛る時も複数を筏のように並べる。
惜春の心にふさわしい菓子だ。
川端道喜

は
な
い
か
だ

Moon over the Rape Flowers

Saikanotsuki, March

"Across the fields of rape flowers,

the sunlight is fading away . . .

The evening moon begins to shine,

conveying the delicate scent from the field."

Soybean-paste flavored bean jam is placed between

yellow *tanesenbei,* rice crackers,

likened to the hazy moon over the field of flowers in bloom.

Kameyaiori

菜花の月　三月

菜の花畑に入日うすれ・・・・

・・・・夕月かかりて匂い淡し

黄色に染めた種煎餅に味噌餡を包み

菜の花畑のおぼろ月に見立てた。

亀屋伊織

さいかのつき

すず

鈴　三月
スズという呼称は　振り鳴らす時の
スズしい音から来ている　ともいう。
振り鳴らして善霊を呼び、悪霊を払う。
身につけてお守りにするのは　そのためか。
亀屋伊織

Suzu, March
The name of *suzu*,
bell, is said to have come from the sound of its ringing.
When we ring the bell,
good spirits are drawn close and bad spirits are driven away.
This might be the reason we wear it as a charm.
Kameyaiori

Bell

Early Bracken

Sawarabi, March

Iwabashiru tarumi no ue no sawarabi no
moe izuru haru to nari ni keru kamo.

Above the dashing water
Of the small waterfall,
The early bracken
Is sprouting.
Ah, spring has come!
In ancient times,
the nobles and the royalty composed
tanka poems on the subject of *sawarabi*,
early bracken. Since then it has become
a symbol of the arrival of spring in Japan
Kameyaiori

早蕨　三月
岩ばしる垂水の上のさわらびの
萌えいづる春となりにけるかも
古代　志貴皇子にうたわれてこのかた
ワラビは日本への春の訪れの象徴だ。
亀屋伊織

さわらび

やなぎ

柳　三月
いまを盛りのサクラの淡紅も美しいが
芽吹いたばかりのヤナギの浅緑も捨てがたい。
芽柳の幾条もの枝が風に吹かれるさまは
見る者の目にしみ、心にしみる。
亀屋伊織

Yanagi, March
The color of cherry blossoms at their peak are splendid.
The light green of just-budding willow
branches is also very beautiful.
The scene of light-green weeping branches blown
in the breeze sinks into the viewers' eyes and minds.
Kameyaiori

Willow

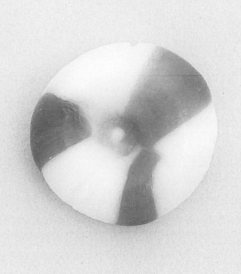

Clog Thong

Hanao, March

Hanao is a thong fastened to a *geta*,
wooden sandal, at its toe.
As I wear the *hanao* between the
first and second toes.
Which spring scene shall I go to see today?

Kameyaiori

花緒　三月
花緒はいわゆる下駄の緒を
下駄先端部に固定する要の止め緒のこと。
花緒を趾の拇指と人斥指のあいだに通して
さて　今日はどんな春景色を見に行こうか。
亀屋伊織

は
な
お

ちござくら

稚児桜　三月
チゴサクラはヤマザクラの一種で
花は白く小さく弁は内側へ反っている。
花の形状と名の愛らしさを表現した
有平糖製の名品といえよう。
亀屋伊織

Chigozakura, March
Chigozakura is a kind of *yamazakura*,
mountain cherry; its blossoms are small and white,
with slightly inward-curving petals.
This confection expresses the loveliness of
the name and the shape of the cherry.
One of the masterpieces made of *aruheitō*,
toffee made of sugar and starch syrup.
Kameyaiori

A Child in a Buddhist Procession
Cherry Blossom

すずめ

雀　三月
「雀化して蛤となる」というのは
中国古代の魔術的天文学による秋の季語だが、
雛祭と貝の縁　また雛を雀の子に通わせ
貝に雀字を取り合わせて　春の菓子とする。
亀屋伊織

Suzume, March
"Suzume kashi te hamaguri to naru",
'A sparrow turns into a clam' is a kigo,
seasonal expression derived from ancient
Chinese astrology.
The clams are eaten and ornaments
made of clam shells are on
display at the Hinamatsuri,
Doll's Festival. The word hina,
baby bird, is associated with chicks of the sparrow.
The confection has a character of suzume,
sparrow, on a clam shell-shaped cake.
A confection of spring.
Kameyaiori

Sparrow

かいづくし

貝づくし　三月
お彼岸の頃の大潮は満干の差が最大で
この頃から　潮干狩がはじまる。
菓子盆の干潟に並んだ貝の中から
好みの貝を採る　これは室内の潮干狩。
亀屋伊織

Kaizukushi, March
The rise and fall of the tides around *Ohigan,*
the spring equinox, are the largest of the year.
People start going shellfish gathering at this time.
From the beach of a tray containing sweets,
one picks up one's favorite shellfish.
This is an indoor shellfish gathering.
Kameyaiori

Shellfish Collection

うのはなむすび

卯の花結び　四月
陰暦四月の雅名卯月は卯の花月のこと
陽暦四月にウノハナはすこし早いが
季節に魁けた趣向の菓子も
もてなしの本義に叶っていよう。
亀屋伊織

Unohana musubi,　April
The elegant name for the Fourth Month in the Chinese
lunar calendar is *Uzuki*, month of deutzia,
which is also called *Unohanazuki*,
deutzia flower's month. It is yet early for the *unohana*
to bloom in the Fourth Month,
but the spirit of serving confections that are
still early for the season may well match
the core meaning of hospitality, that is, to greet the guests.
Kameyaiori

Deutzia Knot

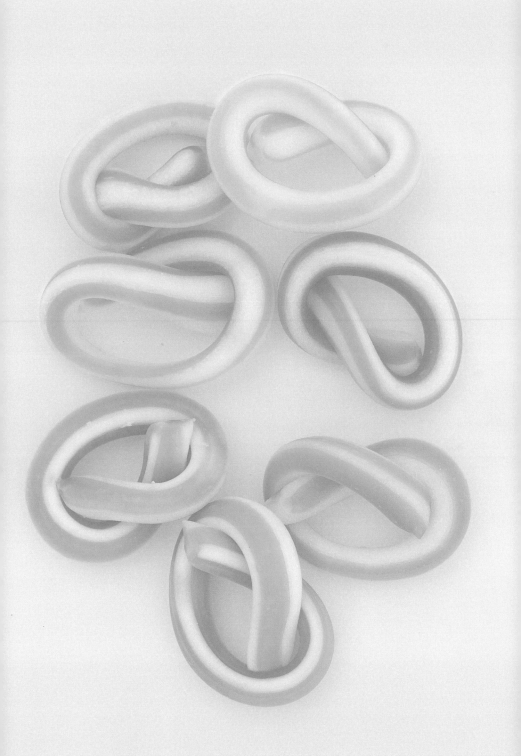

ちょうちょう

蝶々　四月
その年はじめて見るチョウには
確かな春の訪れの実感を覚えるもの、
とくに初蝶と呼んで、いとしんだ。
いかにも伊織らしい春の菓子。
亀屋伊織

Chōchō,　April
The first butterfly seen in the year assures one's mind
of the arrival of the spring.
People called it hatsucho,
first butterfly, with affection.
A vintage spring sweet of Iori.
Kameyaiori

Butterfly

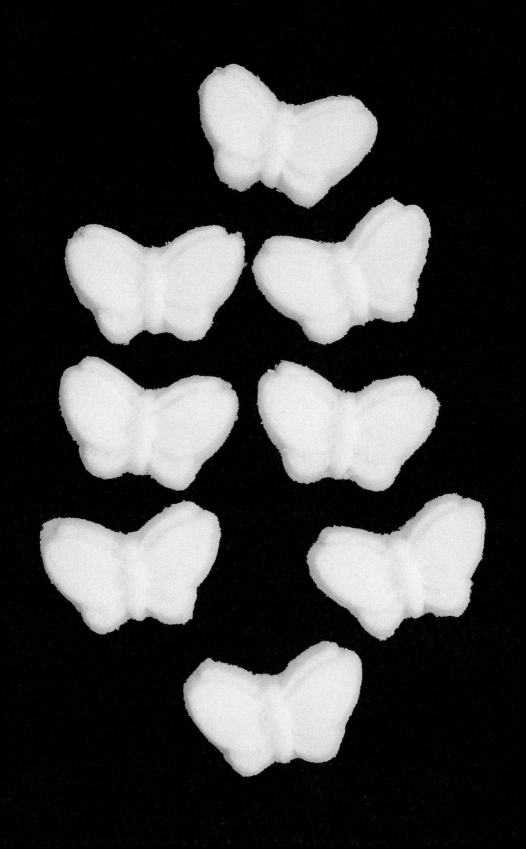

Bamboo Grass Rice Cracker

Sasa senbei, April

The leaves of *takerui*,
trees of the bamboo family,
turn yellow before they grow new bamboo shoots in spring.
We call this phenomenon *take no aki*,
bamboo's autumn. For *sasatake*,
smaller bamboos,
their 'harvesting autumn' occurs in spring, too.
Kameyaiori

笹煎餅　四月
タケ類は地中の筍を育てるため
春になると　葉が黄ばんでくる。
これを竹の秋と言いならわして来た。
ササダケにとっても春は収穫の秋。
亀屋伊織

ささせんべい

Hand-snapped Cherry Twig

Taorizakura, March
Aristocrats of the Heian Period preferred cherry blossoms,
which were native to Japan, over *ume*, plum blossoms,
brought from China.
They would snap off twigs of cherry blossoms,
then decorate their headgear
or their hair with them to show
their love towards the cherry blossoms.
Toraya

手折桜　三月
中国渡りのウメに対する日本の花として
平安時代の貴族が選んだのがサクラ。
彼らはサクラを手折り、または挿頭にして
サクラへの愛を競った。
とらや

たおりざくら

Wizard's Blessing

Senjyu, March
Hinamatsuri, the Doll's Festival, is also called *Momo no Sekku*,
the Seasonal Festival of Peach.
The name came from the legendary *sentō*,
a wizard's peach which was said to ripen
only once every three thousand years in Seiōbo's garden.
The everlasting youth and the eternal life a *sentō*
can bring are considered a blessing for girls' happiness.
Toraya

仙寿　三月
雛祭はまたの名を桃の節句。
西王母の園に三千年に一度実るという
不老長寿の仙桃にあやかり
女の子の倖せを願って名づけた。
とらや

せんじゅ

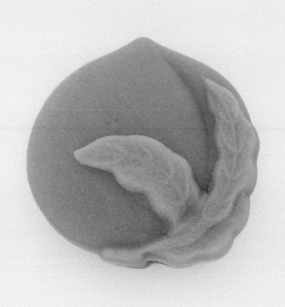

あらしやま

嵐山　三月
桂川の上流　大堰川を前にした嵐山は
吉野山から移した桜が咲き誇る花の名所。
一輪の清楚な桜をかたどる薯蕷饅頭で
洛西の春の情趣を表わした。
とらや

Arashiyama,　March
At its headwaters the River Katsura is called the River Ōi.
Mount Arashi, which is by the river,
is a famous viewing-spot for the magnificent blossoms
of its cherry trees which were transplanted
from Mount Yoshino.
A *jōyomanjū*, bean jam cake wrapped
in a skin containing yam,
is shaped like a single cherry blossom to
express the hearty feeling of spring in Rakusei,
the area east of Kyoto.
Toraya

Mount Arashi

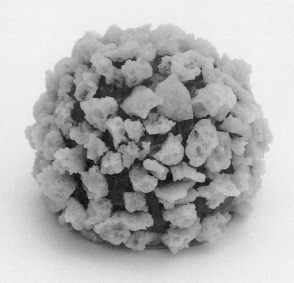

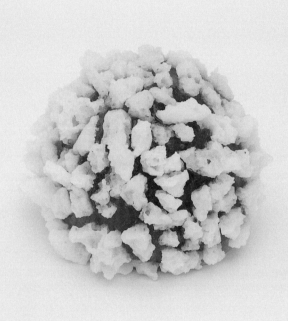

Cherry Blossom Straw Matting

Hanamushiro, March

Hanamushiro is a straw mat laid under the cherry trees
for a cherry-blossom-viewing pot luck party;
it also means the party itself.
We might also be able to say that a *hanamushiro,*
cherry blossom viewing party,
on the scattered petals is a party having
the cherry petals as a *hanamushiro.*

Toraya

花筵　三月
具体的には花見の宴に敷く筵をいうが、
花見の宴そのものも花筵という。
とすれば、散り敷く花びらの上での宴も
花びらを筵にしての宴、花筵といえよう。
とらや

はなむしろ

なたねのさと

菜種の里　三月
野崎参りは　屋形舟で詣ろ
どこを向いても　菜の花盛りー
旧時代の灯（あか）りは菜種油だったから
菜種畑はいたるところに見られた。
とらや

Natane no sato, March
"For a pilgrimage to Nozaki, Nozaki Kannon Temple,
I take a *yakatabune*, houseboat.
Everywhere I look, *na no hana*, the rape flowers,
are in full bloom."
In olden times, it was the rape seed oil that lit the night,
so rape fields were seen everywhere.
Toraya

Village of Rape Flowers

Clam Shape

Hamagurigata, March

Hamaguri, clams, are lovely in shape and color.

They are delicious, too.

No wonder they are ranked at the top among

shellfish and therefore indispensable for wedding dishes

and *Hina* no *Sekku*, Doll's Festival, dishes.

A *jōyomanjū* representing a clam.

Toraya

蛤形　三月

ハマグリは色も形も美しく風味も芳しく

まさに食用貝の中の王者の風格で、

婚礼や雛の節句の料理に欠かせない。

ハマグリを象った薯蕷饅頭である。

とらや

はまぐりがた

とおざくら

遠桜　三月
近々と見るサクラも悪くはないが
遠くから見る風情はまたひとしお。
遠見の桜の濃き、淡き色の階調を
紅と白のそぼろで表現した。
とらや

Tōzakura, March
To have cherry blossoms in view
in front of one's eye is something.
The appearance of cherry blossoms viewed
from afar is especially elegant.
The shade of their deep and pale colors
is expressed by the red and white of *soboro*,
the intricate bits of bean paste.
Toraya

Distant Cherry Blossoms

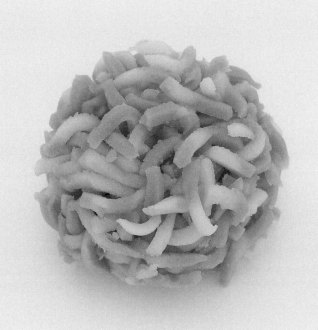

Sado Region

Sadoji, March

Sado Island is where the Emperor Juntoku and
the famous Noh playwright Zeami were sent into exile.
It is a refined island where
one can even find Noh theatres here and there.
The confection embodies,
through the yellow and green colors implying rape flowers,
the peaceful spring that arrives late on the island.

Toraya

佐渡路　三月

順徳天皇や世阿弥が流された佐渡は
能舞台が散在する　雅びの島。
そこに訪れる遅い春ののどかさを
菜の花を思わせる黄と緑で表現。
とらや

さ
ど
じ

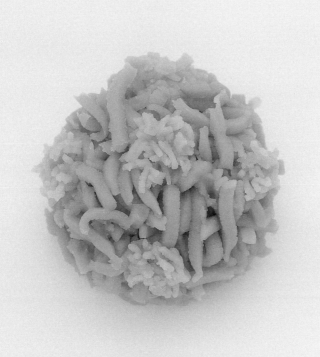

Mount Fuji in Four Seasons Spring

Shiki no fuji Haru, March

Tsukimisō, evening primroses, are said to match Mount Fuji.

Of course, cherry blossoms do, too.

Perhaps, no other flowers match Mount Fiji better than

cherry blossoms in full bloom.

Toraya

四季の富士　春　三月

富士にはツキミソウが似合うというが

もちろん　サクラだって似合う。

いや　満開のサクラ以上に

富士に似合う花はないのではないか。

とらや

しきのふじ　はる

ささごろも

笹衣　四月
ササには防腐効果があるという
黄色く染めた道明寺生地で餡を包み
春の青々とみずみずしいササの葉で
衣のように巻いた爽やかな菓子。
とらや

Sasagoromo, April
Sasa, bamboo grass, is said to have an antiseptic effects.
The bean jam is coated with *dōmyōji kiji*,
paste made of steamed and dried glutinous rice powder,
tinted yellow,
and is wrapped in a fresh bamboo grass leaf like a robe.
A refreshing sweet.
Toraya

Bamboo Grass Robe

Mount Kinugasa Cake

Kinugasaman, April
Among the mountains northwest of Kyoto,
called Kitayama, an especially beautiful one is
Kinugasayama ,Mount Kinugasa.
When its cherry trees are in full bloom,
Kinugasayama, literally Mount Silk Hat,
becomes Hanagasayama, Mount Blossom Hat.
Toraya

衣笠饅　四月
京都の北西に連なる北山の中で
ひときわ美しい衣笠山。
そこにサクラが咲き満ちたら
衣笠山が文字どおり　花笠山に。
とらや

きぬがさまん

Spring Dream

Haru no Yume, April
Chuang Tzu was a Taoist philosopher who lived during the
Warring States Period in ancient China.
After having a dream of a butterfly,
he awoke and did not know whether
it was Tzu dreaming that he was a butterfly
or the butterfly dreaming that he was Tzu.
The confection is made in reference
to the historical fact of Chuang Tzu's dream.
A peaceful confection assuming a butterfly shape.
Toraya

春の夢　四月
古代中国 戦国時代の道家 荘周は
胡蝶の夢を見て目覚め、自分が蝶になったか
蝶が自分になったか わからなくなった という。
荘子の故事に因み 蝶を象ったのどかな菓子。
とらや

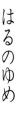

はるのゆめ

みやこのはる

都の春　四月
見わたせば柳桜をこきまぜて
みやこぞ春の錦なりける－
素性法師の名歌のヤナギとサクラとを
緑と紅の二色に染め分けた。
とらや

Miyako no haru, April
Miwatase ba yanagi sakura wo kokimaze te
miyako zo haru no nishiki nari keru
As I look out,
The willows and cherry blossoms
Are mingling together.
The Capital has become
A brocade of spring.
The willows and cherry blossoms in Priest Sosei's
celebrated *tanka* poem are embodied
by the green and crimson colors of the confection.
Toraya

Spring in the Capital

Spring Clock

Harudokei, April
The name is taken from the subject, *toki*,
"time" at the Imperial Court's New Year
Poetry Party held in the twelfth year of the Heisei Era (2000).
Flowers made of bean paste are arranged on yellow *soboro*,
intricate bits of bean paste to a floral clock.
It is the characteristic of Toraya
to endeavor to new confections based on the
contemporary sensibility while
following the old traditions of *wagashi*.
Toraya

春時計　四月
平成十二年の宮中歌会始のお題「時」に因み
黄色いそぼろに煉製の花形で花時計を表わす。
古式ゆかしい菓子の伝統を守るかたわら
新感覚の創作菓子に挑むのもとらやの特徴。
とらや

は
る
ど
け
い

五月　六月

五月中
笹ノ露

壬辰五月十一日写

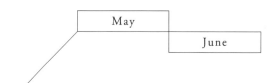

The first day of summer occurs on the first day of the Fourth Month in the Chinese lunar *calendar* which is about May sixth in the solar calendar. The day before summer begins, May fifth, is Children's Day. In ancient times, it was called *Tango no Sekku*, Boy's Festival. A bunch of *shōbu*, irises, were inserted under the eaves, also *koinobori*, a set of carp streamers, was put up on a pole to wish for the wholesome growth of boys. In the tearoom, the hearth changes from *ro*, the sunken hearth, to *furo*, the portable hearth. About ten days into June, it begins to rain and the long rainy season lasts for more than a month. During such a season, we enjoy brewing hot, thick tea and eating a sweet confection to refresh our body and mind which have become musty in the muggy air.

太陽暦五月六日頃が太陰暦四月一日立夏に当たり、暦の上ではこの日から夏に入る。その直前五月五日は子供の日、古くは端午の節句と言い、男の子の健やかな成長を願い、軒に菖蒲を葺き鯉幟を立てる。茶席では湯を沸かす火器が炉から風炉に変わる。六月も十日を過ぎると入梅、一ト月以上の長い雨期がつづく。こういう時こそ甘い菓子を食べ、熱く濃いお茶を喫して、うっとうしい空気の中で黴臭くなった身心を甦らせたくなる。

辛卯孟夏寫

下藍具胭脂曲見ハ誤而下具深シ
今女淺クヌリ又シ曲直或
其上石青掛有如下圖

ちまき

粽　五月
<ruby>泊羅<rt>べきら</rt></ruby>に身を投げた<ruby>屈原<rt>くつげん</rt></ruby>の霊に献じ
供養したのが　粽の起こりという。
室町後期から京の餅座を預かった川端道喜が
茅巻を笹巻に変えて　現在に至っている。
川端道喜

Chimaki, May
The origin of *chimaki*, a rice dumpling
wrapped in bamboo leaves,
was the offering to the spirit of Kutsugen,
Chu Yuan in ancient China, who had committed
suicide by throwing himself into *Bekira*,
the River Miluo Jiang.
Kawabata Dōki, which had been in charge of the
confectionary guild *Mochiza* in Kyoto from
the late Muromachi Period (1392-1573 C.E.),
changed the wrapping from cogon grass
to the present style of a bamboo grass leaf.
Kawabatadōki

Bamboo Grass Leaf Wrap

Wisteria

Fuji, May
Since ancient times,
fuji has been appreciated as a subject of
waka poetry as well as paintings
that lament departing spring and welcome summer.
Look at this gprgeous abstract
created by the Japanese traditional sense of beauty.
Kawabatadōki

藤　五月
フジは春を惜しみ　夏を迎える花として
古来　詩歌にうたわれ　絵に描かれてきた。
日本の伝統的美意識が生んだ
このはなやかな抽象性を見よ。
川端道喜

Green Plum

Aoume, June
Ume, the plum tree,
blooms in February;
in June its fruits become sizable *aoume*, green plums.
This confection is shaped exactly like a fruit
just picked from a tree.
This is a *mochigashi*, rice cake, suitable for the season.
Kawabatadōki

青梅　六月
二月のウメの花は散った後に実を結び
六月にはほどよい大きさの青梅になる。
これをもぎ取った形そのままの
季節に叶った匂いやかな餅菓子だ。
川端道喜

ほととぎすせんべい

時鳥煎餅　五月
春の花　秋の月　冬の雪に対して
夏の季詞の代表がほととぎす。
二枚の種煎餅に味噌餡を挟み
ホトトギスの焼印を押す。
亀屋伊織

Hototogisu senbei, May
Ki no kotoba, seasonal words,
representing the other seasons are *hana*,
cherry blossoms, for spring, *tsuki*, the moon,
for autumn, and *yuki*, snow, for winter.
Misoan, soybean past flavored bean jam,
is placed between *tanesebei*, thin rice crackers,
with a brand mark of summer's little cuckoo on top of it.
Kameyaiori

Little Cuckoo Rice Cracker

たずな

手綱　五月
あおいまつり
葵祭には競べ馬が　馬の轡には手綱が付きもの。
くつわ
左方緋、右方黒の袴の騎手が手にして
はやり立つ馬の動きを制御する。
紅白の有平糖をねじって一結びした。
亀屋伊織

Tazuna,　May
Kutsuwa, the horse's bit, and *tazuna*,
the rein, go together. A jockey wearing a crimson *hakama*,
long pleated Japanese trousers, on the left side,
and a jockey in black *hakama* in the right side are pulling
the reins to control the excited horses.
The twisted red and white *aruheitō*
toffee is made into the shape of a knot.
Kameyaiori

Rein

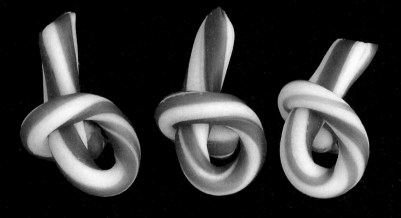

Water

Mizu, May
May is known for its refreshing breezes
and also for the beauty of the water during this season.
There are times when the rain falls
continuously during this month,
called *hashirizuyu*, the early plum rain season.
Kameyaiori

水　五月
風さわやかな五月はまた
水のうつくしい季節でもある。
この月に雨が降りつづくことがあり
走り梅雨と呼ばれる。
亀屋伊織

みず

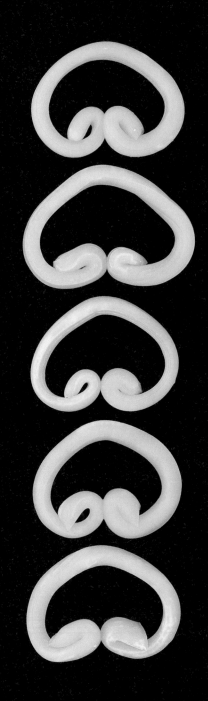

Mallow

Aoi, May

In olden times, when the word *aoi*,
mallow, was mentioned alone,
it referred to *Aoi Matsuri*, the *Aoi* Festival.
From the Imperial Palace in Kyoto,
a parade left for Shimogamo and Kamigamo Shrines;
the Imperial envoy, wore *aoi*,
a mallow, on his headgear.
The confection, using *aruheitō* toffee,
successfully expresses the mallow leaf.
Kameyaiori

葵　五月
その昔　単に祭といえば葵祭のこと。
御所を出て、下鴨・上賀茂両社に向かい
御所に戻る勅使は冠にアオイを飾った。
アオイの葉を有平糖でみごとに表現した。
亀屋伊織

あ
お
い

くつわ

轡　五月
五月五日　京都上賀茂神社の馬場では
古式ゆかしい競べ馬の行事が催される。
その馬の口に含ませるのが轡。
扇面に轡形を打ち出した打ち物だ。
亀屋伊織

Kutsuwa, May
The traditional event *Kurabeuma*,
horse race, is held in the riding ground of
Kamigamo Shrine in Kyoto on May fifth.
Bits are put in the mouths of those horses.
This confection is made by pounding the
steamed and dried powdered glutinous rice
mixed with sugar in a mould to shape
it like a fan with a bit on top of it.
Kameyaiori

Bit

Blue Flag Iris

Ayame, May
The *kanji* or Chinese characters for *ayame*,
blue flag iris, are *shōbu*, sweet flag iris.
But they are not the same plant:
ayame is in the Iris family while *shōbu* is
in the Calla family.
The confection has designed the
blue flag iris in a diamond shape.
Kameyaiori

菖蒲　五月
現在アヤメに菖蒲の漢字を当てるが、
植物学的にアヤメ科のアヤメと
サトイモ科のショウブとは別系統。
アヤメの花を菱形に図案化した。
亀屋伊織

Fringed Pink

Nadeshiko, June
This is one of the seven herbs of autumn,
but it starts to bloom in summer.
It often grows near the riverside and
therefore is also called *kawaranadeshiko*,
riverside fringed pink.
A lovely pale-pink *uchimono*,
a confection made of dried steamed glutinous
rice ground and mixed with sugar
and then pounded in a mould.
Kameyaiori

撫子　六月
秋の七草の一つだが　夏から花をつける。
河原の水近く咲くことが多いことから
カワラナデシコと呼ばれることもある。
淡紅色の打物の可憐な菓子だ。
亀屋伊織

なでしこ

Ditch Reed Rice Cracker

Ashi senbei, June

It is in this season that the reeds growing
at the waterside become vigorous.
In Naniwa (Osaka) they call it *ashi,*
ditch reed, in Edo (Tokyo) *yoshi,*
and in Ise, *hamaogi.*
Ashigoi, a little bittern, and *yoshigoi*
are two names for the same bird;
yoshikiri, reed warbler, and *ashisuzume*
are the same birds, too.
They feed near the *ashihara,*
fields of ditch reeds, and nest to breed.

Kameyaiori

葦煎餅　六月
水辺の葦が勢いを増すのもこの季節。
灘波の葦は江戸の葮、伊勢の浜荻、
アシゴイはヨシゴイ　ヨシキリはアシスズメ、
葦原近く餌をあさり　巣をつくって繁殖する。
亀屋伊織

あしせんべい

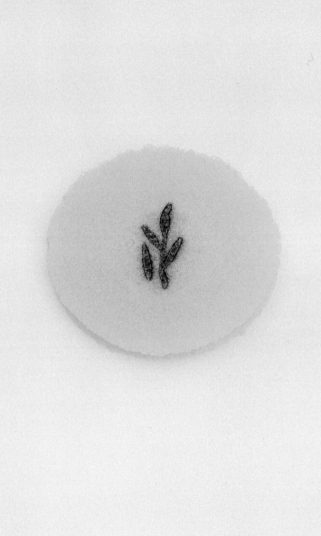

Azalea at the Foot of a Rock

Iwane no tsutsuji, May
Along with *fuji*, wisteria, and *yamabuki*,
Japanese rose, *tsutsuji*, azalea,
is a flower that represents late
spring to early summer in Japan.
Leaves are made of green paste,
while the red *soboro*, intricate bits of bean paste
represent the azalea blooming between the rocks.
Toraya

岩根のつつじ　五月
ツツジはフジ、ヤマブキとともに
晩春から初夏を代表する花。
緑の生地で葉、紅そぼろで花と
岩間に咲くツツジを表現した。
とらや

いわねのつつじ

わ
か
ば
の
か
お
り

若葉のかおり　五月
若葉を吹き抜ける風を薫風という。
樹々は若葉の時が最も香り高い。
緑の道明寺饅頭に楓の焼印を押し
初夏の森のさわやかさを表わす。
とらや

Wakaba no kaori, May
A breeze blowing through *wakaba*,
young leaves, is called *kunpū*, fragrant breeze.
Trees become the most fragrant at the time of young leaves.
The mark of a *kaede*, maple,
is branded on top of the green *dōmyōji manjū*,
a bun wrapped in a skin made of
ground glutinous rice powder.
It embodies the freshness in the early summer forest.
Toraya

Fragrance of Young Leaves

はは
の
かおり

母の薫　五月
五月第二日曜日は母の日。
この日を祝うべく　丸い薯蕷饅頭に
カーネーションの焼印を押し、
花の赤と葉の緑のぼかしを入れた。
とらや

Haha no kaori,　May
The second Sunday in May is Mother's Day.
In order to cerebrate this day,
a brand of a carnation is pressed on a round *jōyomanjū*,
yam bun with bean jam inside.
It is colored with gradations
of the flower's red and the leaf's green.
Toraya

Mother's Fragrance

Blue Flag Cake

Ayameman, May

hototogisu naku ya satsuki no ayamegusa ayame mo
shiranu koi mo suru kana

A little cuckoo is singing,
In the endless rain of Satsuki,
Blue flags are blooming.
I cannot escape
From this dubious love . . .
The *ayamegusa* in this ancient poem
is actually a *shōbu,* sweet flag.
The *ayame* of the *ayamemanjū* is,
of course, blue flag.
Toraya

菖蒲饅　五月
ほととぎす鳴くやさつきのあやめ草
あやめも知らぬ恋もするかな−
古歌にいうあやめ草はショウブのこと
菖蒲饅頭のアヤメはもちろんアヤメ。
とらや

あ
や
め
ま
ん

Blue Flag

Hanaayame, May
Shōbu, sweet flag, belongs to the Calla family
and has quiet flowers.
Hanashōbu, blue flag, and *ayame*, iris,
belong to the Iris family and have vivid flowers.
Shiroazukian, white adzuki bean jam,
is wrapped in the red-colored *dōmyōji*,
and a brand of an iris is pressed on top.
Toraya

花菖蒲　五月
ショウブはサトイモ科で 花が目立たず、
ハナショウブやアヤメはアヤメ科で 花が鮮やか。
紅色の道明寺で 白小豆餡を包み
アヤメの焼印を押した。
とらや

はなあやめ

The Water's Edge

Mizu no hotori, May

We long to visit *mizu* no *hotori*,
the water's edge during the hot summer.
The confection has a mark of *suimon*, the
ripples in the water, on top of the green *dōmyōji* paste
which is sprinkled with *kōrimochi*,
powdered freeze-dried rice cake.
It expresses the tranquility
and the coolness of the shady waterside.

Toraya

水のほとり　五月
暑い夏には水のほとりが恋しいもの。
氷餅をまぶした緑の道明寺生地に
水紋の焼印を押して、木深い水辺の
しずけさとすずしさを表わした。
とらや

みずのほとり

くずやき

葛焼　五月
上質の吉野葛と漉し餡をよく煉り
冷え固まったのち小麦粉をまぶし
鉄板の上で 六方焼きあげたもの。
表面の長方形が氷を思わせて涼しい。
とらや

Kuzuyaki, May
This cake is made by mixing the
high quality Yoshino *Kuzu*, kudzu, and *wasanbontō*,
powdered high quality white sugar,
thoroughly to make the batter.
Then adzukian, adzuki bean jam,
is coated with this batter and is lightly seared
on all six sides on an iron skillet.
The cake's whitish rectangular surfaces remind
us of ice and thus coolness.
Its brilliant purple color matches the reputation of Toraya,
who are renowned for their *yōkan*, jellied bean paste bars.
Toraya

Seared Kudzu Cake

Chinese Robe

Karagoromo, May
The stiff Chinese robe,
More comfortable day by day,
As was my new bride.
How far I seem to have come
As I ponder my journey.
This cake is made in reference
to a *tanka* poem (The tale of is)composed at the water's edge
where *kakitsubata*, rabbit-ear irises, were blooming.
It is colored with the purple and green of the flower.
Toraya

唐衣　五月
唐衣着つつなれにし妻しあれば
はるばる来ぬる旅をしぞ思ふ－
かきつばたの咲く水辺で詠まれた歌（伊勢物語）に因んで
花の紫と葉の緑に染め分けた薯蕷饅頭。
とらや

からごろも

郵 便 は が き

1 7 0 - 8790

038

料金受取人払

料金受取人払

豊島局承認

6880

差出有効期間
平成17年5月
1日まで

東京都豊島区南大塚2-32-4

ピエ・ブックス 行

‖‖·‖·‖‖‖··‖‖‖·‖··‖‖‖‖·‖·‖·‖·‖·‖·‖·‖·‖·‖·‖·‖·‖·‖·‖·‖

このたびは小社の本をお買い上げいただきありがとうございます。新刊案内の送付と今後の
企画の参考とさせていただきますので、お手数ですが各欄にご記入の上お送り下さい。

和菓子

(フリガナ) お 名 前		年齢	性別 **男・女**
ご住所　〒	TEL　　　（　　　）		
e-mail			
ご職業	購入店名		

● いままでに読者カードをお出しいただいたことが　　　1.ある　　2.ない

ご購入書籍名をご記入ください。

1. この本を何でお知りになりましたか
   1. 新聞・雑誌（紙・誌名　　　　　　　　　　）　2. チラシ・ポスター
   3. 友人、知人の話　　　4. 店頭で見て　　　5. プレゼントされた
   6. その他（　　　　　　　　　　　　　　　　　　　　　　　）

2. この本についてのご意見、ご感想をお聞かせください。

　　　　　　　　　　　　　　　　　　　　　　　　　　　　　　　　　　

3. よく購読されている雑誌名をお書き下さい。

●
●
●

4. 今後、小社より出版をご希望の企画、テーマがありましたら、
   ぜひお聞かせください。

● アンケートにご協力いただきありがとうございました。　　　和菓

うじのさと

宇治の里　五月
立春から八十八日目を八十八夜と言い、
この頃から二・三週間が茶摘みの盛り。
飴餡を包んだ求肥にまぶした抹茶が
茶郷宇治の五月をしのばせる。
とらや

Uji no sato,　May
Hachijūhachiya is the eighty-eighth day from *Risshun*,
the first day of spring.
The peak of tea leaf gathering begins around
this time and continues for two to three months.
Matcha, green tea powder, is sprinkled over the *gyūhi*,
starch paste, which wraps the *amean*,
bean jam containing thick malt syrup.
It reminds us of the May season in Uji of Kyoto,
a district famous for its tea production.
Toraya

Village in Uji

Eggplant Cake

Nasubimochi, June

The place of origin for *nasu*, eggplant, is India,
which came to Japan from China.
In the first Japanese encyclopedia, "*Wamyōruijūshō*",
written in the Heian Period, it is called *nasu* or *nasubi*,
eggplant. The white bean jam is wrapped in *uirō*,
sweet rice dough, containing black sesame seeds.
It is shaped as a plump, round, white eggplant.

Toraya

なすび餅　六月

ナスはインド原産で　中国経由で渡来、
平安時代の『和名抄』に「茄子　奈須比」とある。
黒胡麻入りの白餡を外郎（ういろう）で包んで
丸くふくよかな白ナスを象った。
とらや

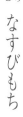
なすびもち

Young Willow   Translucent Kudzu Cake

Suisenaoyagi,   June
A high quality kudzu powder produced in Yoshino of Nara,
Yoshino *kuzu,* is dissolved in water with sugar,
and boiled to make a thick translucent paste.
A bean jam cake wrapped in this kudzu paste
is called *Suisenmanjū.*
This is its variation in an *aoyagi,*
young willow leaves, color.
The coolness of *suisenman*
is a treat in the summer season.

Toraya

水仙青柳　六月
上質の吉野葛を水で溶き、砂糖を加え
煮て煉り固めた葛皮でこし餡を包んだ。
世にいう葛饅頭で　これは青柳色。
涼味ある水繊饅は夏期　最も喜ばれる。
とらや

すいせんあおやぎ

なつぎく

夏菊　六月

キク科には種類が多く　初夏から
咲きはじめる小ぶりのナツギクもその一種。
菊の瀬戸型に黄色い粟羊羹を流し込み、
暑さに負けず咲く花の可憐さを表現した。
とらや

Natsugiku,　June
There are a variety of species in *kiku*,
the chrysanthemum family.
Natusgiku, summer chrysanthemum,
which begins to bloom with a comparatively
small flower in early summer,
is one of them. The confection is made
by pouring yellow *awayōkan*,
chestnut bean jelly, into a *setogata*,
a mould for shaping the confection.
It expresses the loveliness of a tiny flower blooming
in spite of the heat.
Toraya

Summer Chrysanthemum

わ
か
ば
か
げ

若葉蔭　六月
青葉若葉のかげには水があり
水にはキンギョが無心に泳いでいる。
梅雨どきのうっとうしさを忘れる
涼しい菓子で　若い世代の人気も高い。
とらや

Wakabakage,　June
Behind the shade of the *aoba*,
fresh green leaves, and *wakaba*,
young leaves, there is water, where *kingyo*,
goldfish, are swimming innocently.
This confection makes us forget the dullness of the *tsuyu*,
plum rain season.
This sweet is popular among young people,too.
Toraya

Young Leaves' Shade

みなづき

水無月　六月
水無月の夏越の祓する人は
ちとせ　　　　なごし　はらへ
千歳の命延ぶといふなり－
氷を象った新粉製三角形の上に
かたど
邪気祓いの煮小豆を散らす。
とらや

Minadzuki, June
Those who take part
In the purification rite
Of the Month of Water,
Of them it is said, life increased
For a thousand years.
The triangular cake, representing a piece of ice,
is made from *shinko*, rice flour.
On top it has adzuki beans,
which have the power to scare away the evil.
Toraya

The Water's Month

Mount Fuji in Four Seasons   Summer

Shiki no fuji Natsu, June

Mount Fuji in summer does not have snow on it,

so it looks rather ordinary.

But the power we feel from nature itself can still be felt.

In a series of Hokusai's *"Fugaku Sanjūrokkei* "and

"Fugaku Hhyakkei," "The 36 views of Mount Fuji

" and "The 100 views of Mount Fuji",

there are many masterpieces depicting summer,

such as *"Gaifūkaisei",*

"Southern Wind on a Fine Day" and *"Sankahakuu",*

"Shower on the Mountainside."

Toraya

四季の富士　夏　六月

夏の富士は山肌に雪もなく

一見平凡だが　自然本来の迫力に富む。

北斎の富獄三十六景・百景にも

凱風快晴　山下白雨など　夏の傑作が多い。

とらや

しきのふじ　なつ

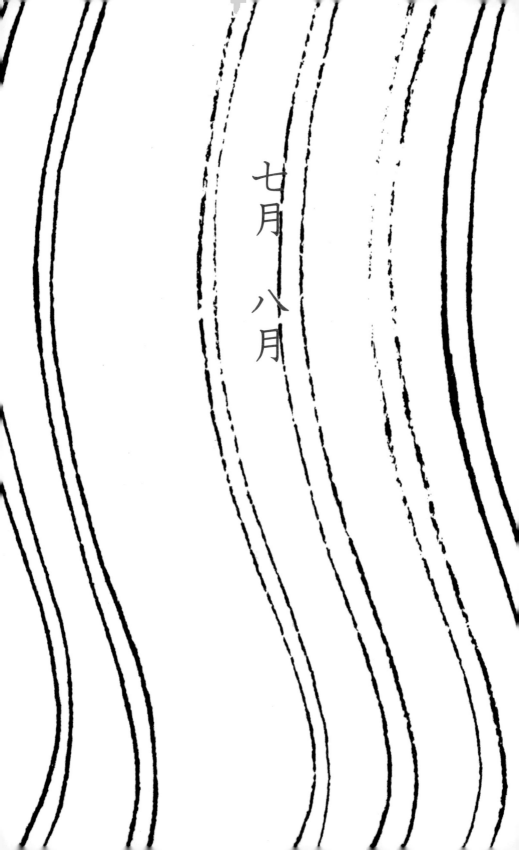

七月

八月

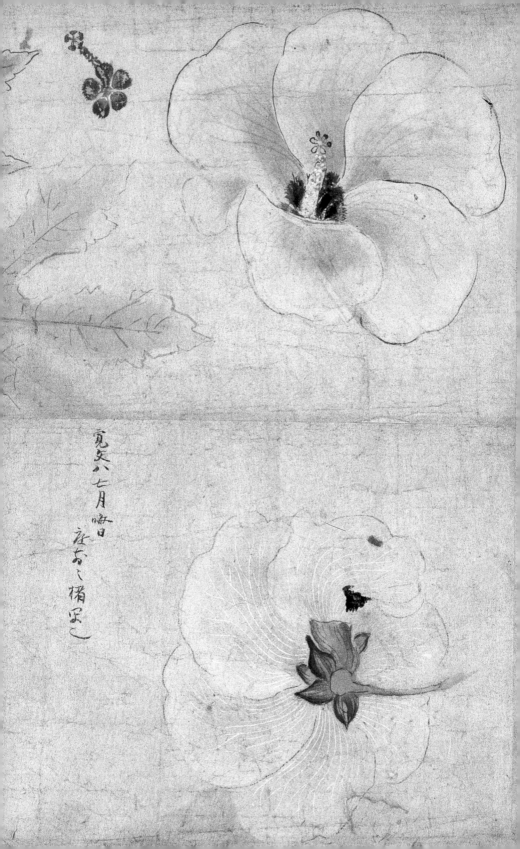

寛文八七月晦日
庭右ニ楷写之

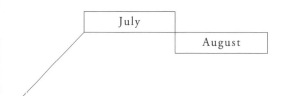

July	
	August

In the calendar July is late summer; with *Risshū*, the first day of autumn, around August 8th, autumn begins. According to our experience, however, the period of high summer begins with the end of *tsuyu*, the plum rain season, and continues till the end of August. A tea ceremony usually begins at noon, but during this season *asacha* morning tea ceremony, is often held at six o'clock in the morning to avoid the midday heat. *Tanabata*, the Star Festival, was formerly celebrated on the Seventh day of the Seventh Month in the Chinese lunar calendar, already autumn in solar calendar, but now it has shifted to July which is still summer. During the sixty days of high summer, it is the cool type of confectionery that is favored most.

暦の上では七月は晩夏、八月八日頃の立秋からは秋ということだが、実感の上では梅雨明けから八月中旬までが盛夏、八月も下旬になってようやく晩夏というのが正直なところではないか。茶席はふつう正午から始まるが、この時期は日中の暑さを避けて午前六時からの朝茶が盛んだ。七夕はほんらい旧暦七月七日で秋の行事だったが、現在では新暦で夏の行事に変わった。とにかく炎暑酣わの六十日余、菓子ももっぱら涼しげなものが喜ばれる。

238

菊をいろこ
元二寸あり大き

The Milky Way

Ama no gawa, July
Yellow and red *dango*, rice dumplings, with *koshian*,
strained bean jam, inside are skewered on a green bamboo skewer.
The dumplings represent the stars *Kengyū*, Altair, and *Shokujo*, Vega.
The straightness of the skewer reminds us of the lines connecting
the stars in a constellation.
The name, *Ama no Gawa*, River of Heaven,
matches the Star Festival and its beauty.
Kawabatadōki

天の川　七月
黄色と紅色の漉し餡入りの団子を
青竹の串に刺して、牽牛・織女の二星を表わす。
真直な串が星座の星々を結ぶ線を思わせる
天の川の名も七夕に叶って、美しい。
川端道喜

あ
ま
の
が
わ

はづき

葉月　八月
旧暦八月の雅名葉月は落葉月の略。
新暦の感覚では葉の茂る月の趣き。
漉し餡入りのみずみずしい葛菓子を
しっとり濡れた笹の葉に包んだ。
川端道喜

Hazuki,　August
Hazuki, the elegant name of the Eighth Month
in the Chinese lunar calendar is an abbreviation of *Ochibazuki*,
the falling leaves' month. According to our sense,
August is the month of thickly growing leaves.
A fresh *kuzugashi*, a confection made of kudzu,
with *koshian*, strained bean jam,
inside is wrapped in a moistened *sasa*, bamboo grass leaf.
Kawabatadōki

Leaf Month (Eighth Month)

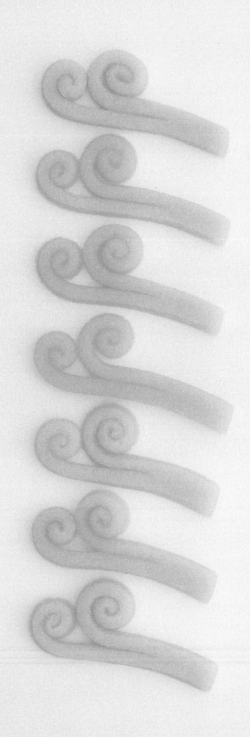

さざなみ

さざ波　七月
さざ波の立つのは湖か　海か、
いずれ　微風が吹きわたるのだろう。
菓子自体の美しさもさることながら
菓名の美しさにも注目。
亀屋伊織

Sazanami,　July
Sazanami, ripples, appear on the surface of a *mizuumi*,
a lake, or a *shioumi*, an ocean.
Wherever they appear a breeze must be blowing.
Not only is the beauty of the confection
itself notable but the beauty of
its name should also be noted.
Kameyaiori

Ripples

Water

Mizu, July

More than thirty of the ninety days of *sanka*,
three summers (early, middle, and late summer),
are made up of *tsuyu*, the plum rain season.
Thus we might be able to say that even the
scorching summer season is a season of water.
With the blessing of *tsuyu*, plum rain season,
the rice seedlings can be planted,
and the vegetables and fruits grow freshly.

Kameyaiori

水　七月

三夏九十日のうち　三十日余が梅雨、
炎暑の夏はまた　水の季節でもある。
梅雨のめぐみのもと　田植がおこなわれ、
野菜や果物がいきいきと育つ。

亀屋伊織

みず

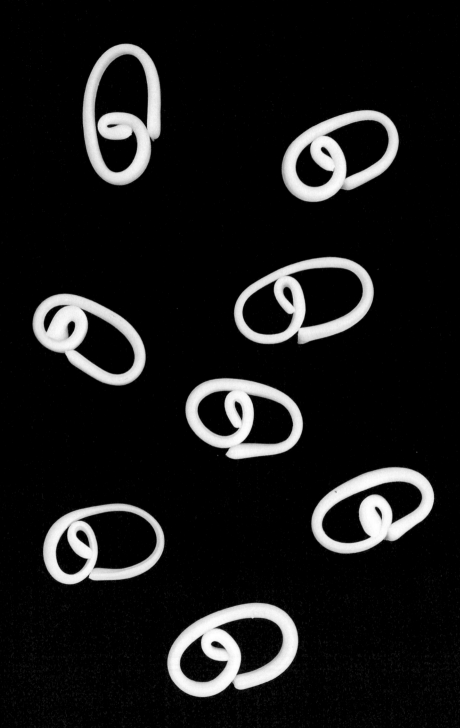

かん
ぜ
すい

観世水　七月
観世水とは渦を巻く水のかたち
能楽家元・観世太夫の紋所ゆえの呼び名。
動きのある分だけ　涼しげに見え
夏の盛りの菓子として喜ばれる。
亀屋伊織

Kanzesui, July
Kanzesui, Kanze water,
is in the shape of water making a whirl.
This was the shape of the crest of Kanzedayū,
the head of the school of Kanze Noh,
and so the confection was named after him.
The movement in this shape makes it look cool.
The confection is a delight in the high summer season.
Kameyaiori

Whirlpool

Rough Rocky Beach

Ariso, August
At the end of summer,
the waves seem to be getting higher and higher,
washing the rocky beach.
Such a beach is called *araiso*, rough rocky beach.
Also the pattern of a carp jumping through the waves
is called *araiso moyō*, *araiso* pattern,
which has been abbreviated as *araiso*.
Kameyaiori

荒磯　八月
夏の終わり　目に見えて高くなった波が
荒あらしく打ちよせる磯浜を荒磯という。
また　波間に跳るコイを織り出した模様も
荒磯模様　略して荒磯という。
亀屋伊織

あ
お
か
え
で

青楓　七月
秋の紅葉したカエデとはこと変わり
夏の青々としたカエデは清爽そのもの。
新緑の頃から夏を通して用いられる打物で
水の意匠の菓子と取り合わせられることが多い。
亀屋伊織

Aokaede, July
The green maple leaves in summer have a different beauty
from the crimson ones in autumn;
they are themselves very refreshing.
This *uchimono*, moulded cake,
is served from the time of young green leaves
throughout the summer.
It is often combined with sweets with a water motif.
Kameyaiori

Green Maple

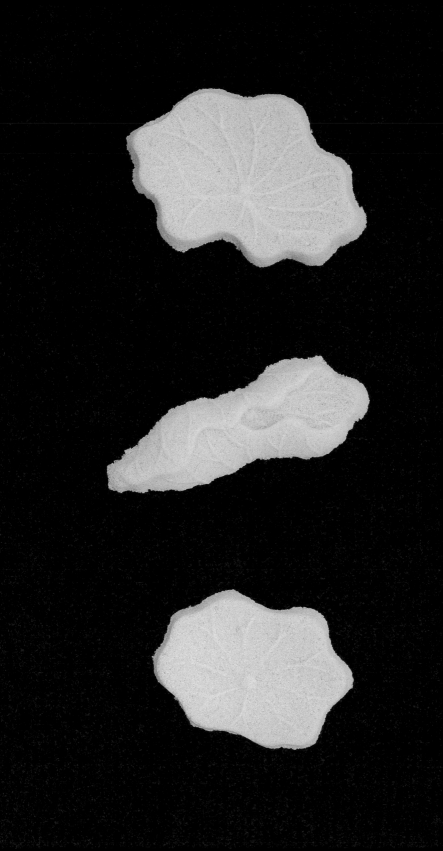

Arrowhead

Omodaka, July

The characteristics of *omodaka*, arrowhead,
which grows in mountain streams and rice fields
are its three-*petalled* white flowers and the
arrowhead-shaped leaves growing on thin stems.
Uchimono, a confection made by pounding a mixture
of steamed and dried powdered glutinous rice
and sugar in a mould, depicts its quaint leaf.
It is usually served with a water-shaped confection.
Kameyaiori

沢瀉　七月
沢や田などに自生するオモダカは
細い茎の先の矢尻型の葉と三弁の白い花が特徴。
その趣ある葉を象って、打物にした。
水などと取り合わせられることが多い。
亀屋伊織

お
も
だ
か

は
ち
す

蓮　七月
はちす葉のにごりにしまぬ心もて
なにかは露を玉とあざむく－
僧正遍照の歌には花はうたわれていないが
ハスの花は夏の水辺の花の中の女王。
亀屋伊織

Hachisu,　July
Hachisuba no nigori ni shima nu kokoro mote
nanika wa tsuyu wo tama to azamuku
The lotus leaf's heart
By the muddy water
Undefiled.
Yet can deceive us into seeing
A crystal in a dewdrop!
Although its flower is not mentioned,
in this poem by Sōjō Henjō,
the lotus flower is the queen of waterside flowers in summer.
Kameyaiori

Lotus

ほたるせんべい

蛍煎餅　七月
夏の夜の鳥の代表がホトトギスなら、
夏の夜の虫の代表はホタルだろうか。
ゆっくりと動く　熱を伴わない冷たい光が
うっとうしい梅雨時の涼味を呼ぶのだろう。
亀屋伊織

Hotaru senbei, July
If the representative of the night birds
in summer is *hototogisu,* little cuckoo,
the representative insect might be *hotaru,* firefly.
The fireflies' cool slowly swaying lights
do not generate heat;
they make us feel the coolness in the
muggy nights during *tsuyu,* plum rain season.
Kameyaiori

Firefly Rice Cracker　　　　　　258

A Round Fan

Uchiwa, July

Uchiwa, a round fan,
looks more informal than *sensu*, a folding fan.
It may not be a good idea to fan
oneself with the confection,
but with this one we can sense
the hospitality of the host wishing for us to relax.

Kameyaiori

団扇　七月
どこか改まった感じの扇に対して
団扇はいかにもくつろいだ感じ。
菓子の団扇ではあおぐわけにはいくまいが
くつろいでほしい主の心は伝わってくる。
亀屋伊織

うちわ

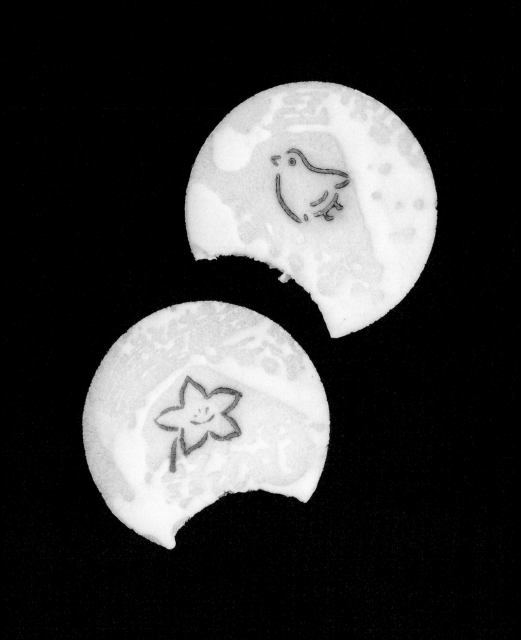

Waterfall Rice Cracker

Taki senbei, July

Waterfalls are there all year round.
The reason for their inclusion in summer *kikotoba*,
seasonal words, is due to their refreshing appearance.
On a rectangular rice cracker, *shirosatōmitsu*,
white sugar syrup,
is placed to give an effect of spray from a waterfall.
kameyaiori

瀧煎餅　七月
瀧は四季を通じてあるものだが
清涼な眺めから夏の季詞とする。
長方形の煎餅に白粗糖蜜を流して
瀧しぶきの趣きを出している。
亀屋伊織

たきせんべい

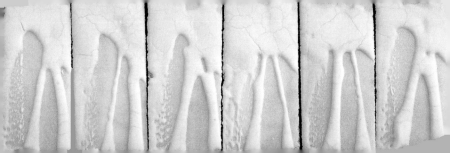

いとまき

糸巻　七月
七夕はまたの名を乞巧典（きっこうでん）とも言い、
裁縫の上達を願う女の祭でもあった。
裁縫の裁は鋏、縫は針と糸、
糸巻は乞巧典のシンボルマーク。
亀屋伊織

Itomaki, July
Another name for *Tanabata*,
the Star Festival, was *Kikkōden*,
the festival for women who wished
for progress in their *saihō*, sewing.
The *sai* of *saihō* means scissors;
hō stands for thread and needles.
Itomaki, a spool, is the symbol
for the *Kikkōden* Festival.
Kameyaiori

Spool   264

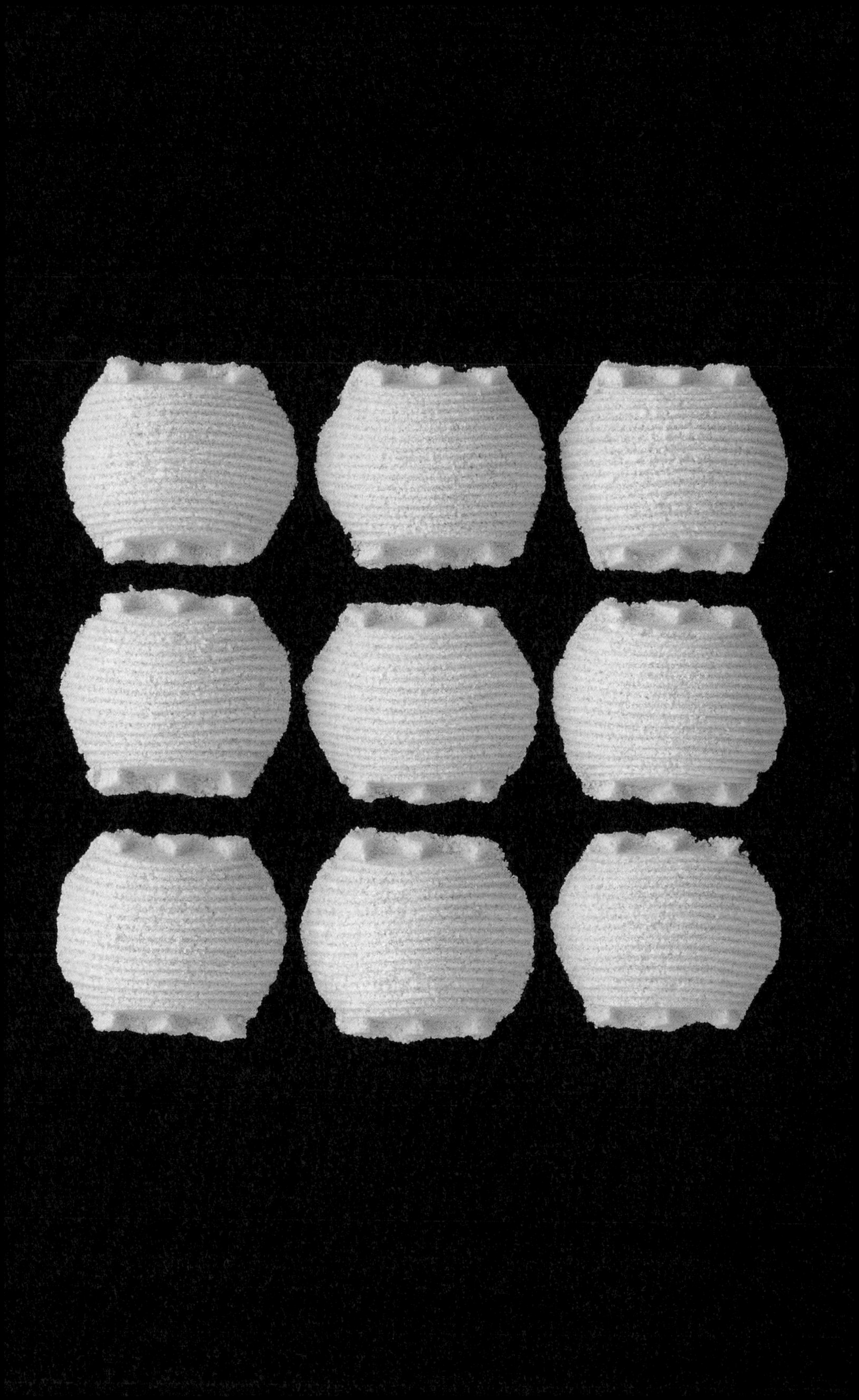

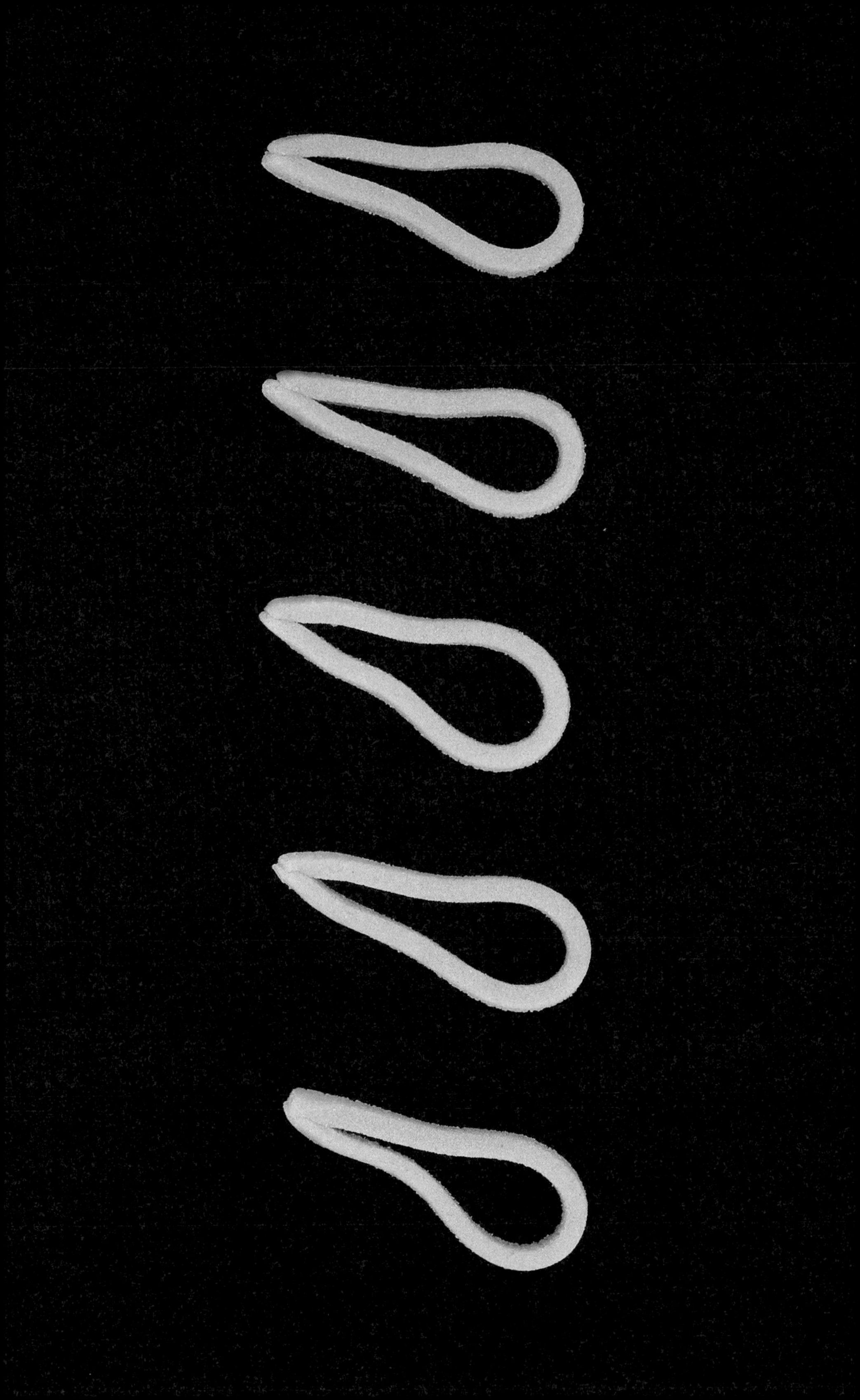

ききょう

桔梗　八月

秋の七草の「あさがほ」というのは
じつはキキョウのことだという。
そのすがすがしい形と色から
盆供の花に最も喜ばれる。

亀屋伊織

Kikyō, August

It is said that the *asagao*, morning-glory,

listed as one in *aki* no *nanakusa,*

seven herbs of autumn,

was actually a *kikyō*, Japanese bellflower.

Its refreshing color and shape make *kikyō*

the most favored offering flower at the Bon Festival.

Kameyaiori

Japanese Bellflower

ゆ
う
が
お

夕顔　八月
朝咲く朝顔に対して　夕方咲くことから
ユウガオと呼ばれるが　植物学的にはウリ科。
その実のフクベを線描きした塩梅式（あんばいしき）に
緑色の洲浜（すはま）で仕上げている。
亀屋伊織

Yūgao, August
Yūgao, bottle gourd, which means 'evening face'
acquired its name from blooming in the evening,
while *asagao,* morning-glory,
which means 'morning face' got its name
from blooming in the morning.
Botanically, it belongs to *urika,*
the melon family.
An outline of a gourd is made with *suhama,*
a rice cake sweetened with sugar and
wheat gluten, which is seasoned with *anbai,*
salt and sour plum juice.
Kameyaiori

Bottle Gourd

Summer Frost Translucent Kudzu Cake

Suisen natsu no shimo, July

It is unusual to have frost in summer,

but this was named after the line,

"*Tsuki heisa wo terasu kaya no shimo*",

"The moon shines on the flat sand field,

summer's frost",

in a poem composed by Hakukyoi, Pai Lo-tien.

The image is represented by a type

of confection called *suisen,*

a bean jam cake with the translucent skin made

of sweetened kudzu paste.

Toraya

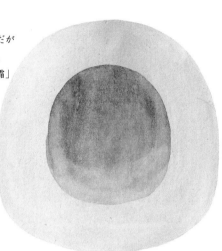

水仙夏の霜　七月

夏に霜が降りるのは天候異常だが

これは白居易の詩の一行から。

「月平沙を照らす　夏の夜の霜」

その意を水繊饅で表わした。

とらや

すいせんなつのしも

Morning Light

Ashita no hikari, July

The morning sunlight on a morning in July,
after the dull *tsuyu*, plum rain season,
is over, is incomparably beautiful.
The freshness of an early hour before the day's
work begins is represented by the color and shape of asagao,
a morning glory, wet with the morning dewdrops.

Toraya

朝の光　七月
うっとうしい梅雨が明けた後の
七月の朝の光は　比べるものなく美しい。
暑い一日が始まる前のすがすがしさを
露を含んだアサガオの色と形で表わした。
とらや

あしたのひかり

Green Pear

Aonashi, July
The records of the *chakai*, tea ceremony,
held during the Momoyama Period tell that *nashi*,
pears, were often served as confectionery.
Bean jam is wrapped in a green *yōkan*,
jellied bean paste,
and is sprinkled with poppy seeds
to give a texture of *nashiji*, pear-skin lacquer.
Toraya

青梨　七月
ナシは桃山時代の茶会で　しばしば
菓子として使われていた記録が残る。
葛を使った緑の水羊羹で餡を包み
芥子の実を散らし梨子地とした。
とらや

あおなし

まつばぼたん

松葉牡丹　七月
マツバボタンは炎暑つづきの盛夏
日なたにいきいきと咲きつづける。
みずみずしい枝葉を緑のきんとんで
咲きつづける小花を紅琥珀糖で表わした。
とらや

Matsubabotan, July
Matsubabotan, moss rose,
blooms vividly under the scorching sun
during the high summer.
The fresh green of its stems and leaves are made of *kinton*,
and the little flowers that
keep blooming of crimson *kohakutō*,
sweet jelly made of agar.
Toraya

Moss Rose

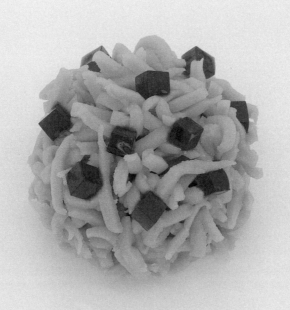

Sunflower

Himawari, July

Himawari, sunflower,
is ranked as the queen of the summer flowers.
The seeds at the center are made of *koshian*,
strained bean jam, and the petals are made of yellow *soboro*,
intricate bits of bean paste.
This is one of Toraya's that matches
the sensibility of the present time.
Toraya

向日葵　七月
ヒマワリは夏の花の女王の位。
花芯の種子の部分をこし餡で
花びらの部分を黄色のそぼろで表現、
これもとらやの新感覚の菓子の一つ。
とらや

ひ
ま
わ
り

The Milky Way

Ama no gawa, July
The legend of the two stars in love
crossing the river of light across the summer sky
to meet once a year is the most beautiful romance
that human beings have ever created.
A summer confection depicting
the night sky and the river of light.
Toraya

天の川　七月
夏の夜空に横たわる光の河を越えて
恋する二星が年に一度逢うという伝説は
人間が考え出した最も美しいロマンのひとつ。
夜空と光の河を表現した夏らしい菓子。
とらや

あ
ま
の
が
わ

Thousand Years Bamboo Grass

Chitose no sasa, August

Sasa, bamboo grass,

remains unchanged in color under the scorching sun;

thus it is regarded as a symbol of eternal youth and life,

as well as the prosperity of one's descendants.

In a classical bamboo grass shaped mould made of china,

yōkan, jellied bean paste,

mixed with *matcha*, green tea power,

is poured.

Toraya

千歳の笹　八月
ササは炎天下にも色を変えず
不老長生　子孫繁栄の象徴。
古典的な笹を象った瀬戸型に
抹茶入りの水羊羹を流し込んだ。
とらや

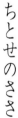

ゆうすずみ

夕涼み　八月
暑い夏の日も日暮れがたになると
涼風が立って　しのぎやすくなる。
縁側や屋外に出ての夕涼みの風情を
白と水色のそぼろで表現した。
とらや

Yūsuzumi, August
When the evening comes,
a hot day becomes bearable with the arrival of a cool breeze.
The appearance of people enjoying the evening cool
on the veranda or outside is embodied
by white and pale-blue *soboro*,
intricate bits of bean paste.
Toraya

Evening Cool

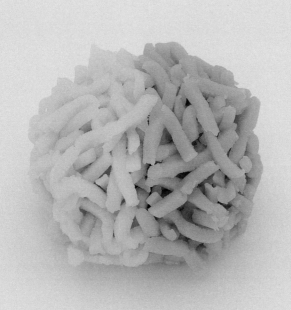

ささぐり

ささ栗　八月
ササグリのササとは小さいこと
柴栗の別名がささ栗である。
栗のいがのあいだから実が弾けるさまを
さみどりのそぼろと餡で表わした。
とらや

Sasaguri, August
Sasa in *sasaguri* means' small'.
Shibaguri, a small chestnut,
is another name for *sasaguri*.
The moment the chestnut bursts open
is depicted with fresh green *soboro* and *an*,
bean jam.
Toraya

Small Chestnut

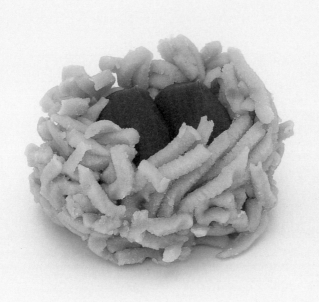

うづらまき

うづら巻　八月
鶉巻とは白い革を細縄で巻き
くすぶらせて　縄模様をつけたものをいう。
蒸した道明寺生地に白小倉餡を巻いた
独持の風味が喜ばれる。
とらや

Uzuramaki, August
A method of printing a rope pattern
on white leather by coiling a thin rope and
smoldering it is called *uzuramaki,* a quail roll.
The roll's unique taste combining *shiroazukian,*
white adzuki bean jam, with the *dōmyōji,*
paste made of ground glutinous rice powder,
is a delight.
Toraya

Quail Roll

Alga Flower Translucent Kudzu Cake

Suisen mizumo no hana, August
In the summer, the stems of the fresh water algae growing
in lakes and ponds reach above the water's
surface with tiny pale flowers between
their leaves.
The confection expresses the delicacy of the
flower using *suisenmanjū,*
a cake coated with a translucent kudzu.
Toraya

水仙水藻の花　八月
湖や沼など　淡水に生じる藻は夏
水底から伸びた茎が　水面から出て
葉のあいだに淡い小花をつける。
そのやさしい風情を水繊饅にした。
とらや

すいせんみずものはな

Watermelon

Suika, August

The representative summer fruit is *suika*,
watermelon, above all.
Cutting the well-chilled watermelon into big portions,
holding it in both hands,
and getting one's teeth into it is an irresistible feeling!
The confection has successfully abstracted the essence
of a section of watermelon.

Toraya

西瓜　八月
夏のくだものの代表はやはりスイカ。
よく冷えたやつをざっくり切って
両手に持って食べる感覚はこたえられない。
スイカの断面を抽象化した。
とらや

す
い
か

九月

十月

唯莖具
アンシ曲ロスベ

| September | |
| | October |

It is autumn. In the calendar, September is considered mid-autumn, and October late autumn. However, it might be easier to understand September as the month of *nowaki,* typhoons, and *tsukimi,* moon viewing, and October as the month for *minori,* the harvest, and *momiji,* tinted leaves. The severe heat gradually lessen after the passing of *nowaki* around the dates of *Nihyakutōka* and *Nihyakuhatsuka,* respectively the two hundred and tenth and two hundred and twentieth days after *Risshun,* the first day of spring. The air gets cooler and we look up at the *meigetsu,* the harvest moon, in the clear night sky. In October, the rice ripens in the fields and various fruits ripen in the hills and valleys; flowering es grasses bloom in the meadows, and the tree leaves change their color. Then *hatsushigure,* the first winter shower, falls over the colored leaves and grasses. The confections show a rich variety in reflecting the season. They represent such things as the moon, a grass flower, and a tinted leaf.

秋である。暦の上では九月が中秋、十月が晩秋ということになるが、九月を野分（颱風）と月見の月、十月を実りと紅葉の月とした方がわかりやすいかもしれない。きびしい残暑も九月に入ると、二百十日、二百二十日の野分の通過で涼しくなり爽やかな夜空に名月を仰ぐ。十月に入ると、田んぼの稲、山野の果物が実り、野の草が花を咲かせ、木の葉が色づく。やがて紅葉・草葉の上に初時雨が来る。菓子も季節を映して、月、草の花、紅葉・・・・・と彩りに富む。

初茸
紫土具
弓に墨を
作づ葉

298

菊花数品

赤初茸
辛卯九
丁字
具維
付加曲

黄丹具ヨシ付

ヨシ付中粉曲

黄シメシ
墨カスリ
コル作土佐
コル墨油
土佐白ノ十

黄丹具
胡粉
込

黄丹具ヨシ付

Japanese Bush Clover Cake

Hagi no mochi, September
With the picture of flowery fields and hills covered with *hagi,*
Japanese bush clover, in mind, the *mochigome,* glutinous rice,
and *uruchimai,* nonglutinous rice,
are mixed and steamed together and then pounded.
It is shaped and wrapped with adzukian,
adzuki bean jam. The cake is also known as *ohagi,*
rice dumpling covered with bean jam.
This is what Kawabata Dōki offered to the
Emperor every morning as the *oasamono,*
Emperor's morning cake.
Kawabatadōki

萩の餅　九月
野山に咲き乱れるハギを意 (こころ) に
糯米 (もちごめ) と粳米 (うるち) とを合わせて蒸し上げ
潰して小豆餡で包んだ　いわゆるお萩 (はぎ) 。
道喜が天皇に毎朝献った御朝物 (おあさもの) がこれ。
川端道喜

はぎのもち

いのこもち

亥の子餅　十月
陰暦十月亥日に餅をつく中国の風習に準い
わが国でも餅をつき　亥の子餅と名づけた。
茶の湯ではこの日に炉を開き、亥の子餅を食べる。
糯米と小豆を半づきした肌は　猪の子を思わせる。
川端道喜

Inoko mochi,　October
Following the Chinese custom of pounding steamed rice
into cake on the Day of the Boar
in the Tenth Month in the Chinese lunar calendar,
we also make rice cake on this day and call it *Inoko Mochi*,
rice cake of the Boar.
In *Cha* no *yu*, tea ceremony,
they open the sunken hearth and eat *Inoko Mochi*.
The texture of the confection's half-pounded glutinous rice
and adzuki beans remind us of a boar.
Kawabatadōki

Boar Day Cake

きく、は

菊、葉　九月

キクという日本語は中国音から来ている。

つまり　中国からの上代の輸入植物。

古代中国での評価をそのまま輸入して

キクは日本では　現在にいたるまで「めでたさ」の象徴。

亀屋伊織

Kikuha,　September

The sound of the word *kiku*,

chrysanthemum, came from the Chinese pronunciation,

indicating that this plant was imported from China.

Kiku came to Japan in the Nara Period.

In Japan it retained the esteem it had earned in China,

of a *medetasa*, 'propitious sign'.

It has kept this regard down to the present day.

Kameyaiori

Chrysanthemum Leaf

Rabbit Rice Cracker

Usagi senbei, September
"Rabbits, rabbits, where are they looking and jumping?
To the fifteenth-day moon, they are looking and jumping!"
As in the children's song,
it is our custom to see a rabbit in the moon.
Kameyaiori

兎煎餅　九月
うさぎ　うさぎ　何見てはねる
十五夜お月さま　見てはねるー
童謡でうたわれるとおり、
月面にウサギを見るのは　日本人の習いだ。
亀屋伊織

うさぎせんべい

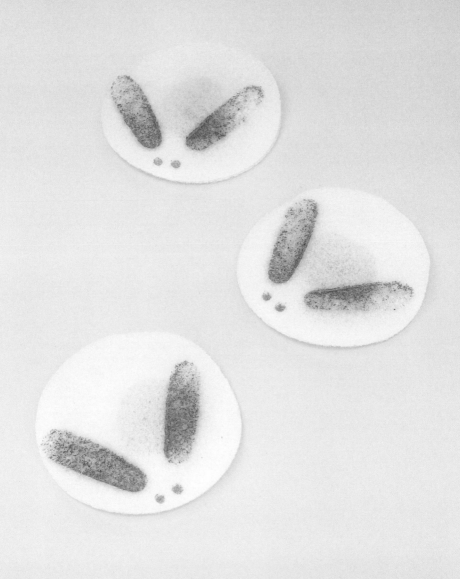

Green Soybean

Edamame, September
The thirteenth day in the Ninth Month
in the Chinese lunar calendar is called *Nochi no Tsuki,*
thirteenth-day moon.
The appreciation of this aspect of the moon
is something not found in China
where the habit of moon viewing originated.
It is a custom unique to Japan.
Because the soybeans harvested at this season
are offered to the moon,
it is also called *Mame Meigetsu,*
the Soybean Moon. A nostalgic *kidai* or seasonal word.
Kameyaiori

枝豆　九月
陰暦九月十三日の月を後の月と言い
これは本家の中国にはない　日本だけの風習。
この頃実る枝豆を供えて月を祀るので
豆名月というなつかしい季題がある。
亀屋伊織

えだまめ

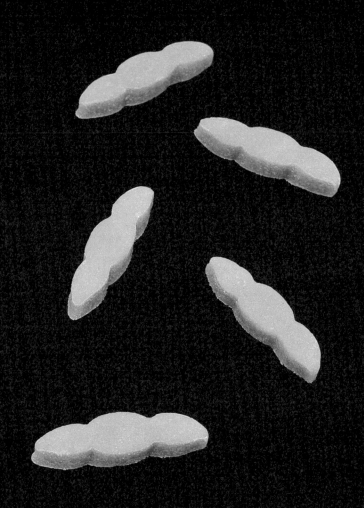

Rice Plant Rice Cracker

Ine senbei, October
The hero and heroine of the autumn rice fields are,
of course, the *inasuzume,*
sparrows coming to peck at the ripe grains.
A brand mark of rice leaves and rice heads
is pressed on the *senbei,* rice crackers.
These designs were suggested over a period
of time by customers of the confectionery
who were painters and tea masters.
Kameyaiori

稲煎餅　十月
秋の田の主人公はもちろん熟稲。
稲葉と稲穂の焼印を煎餅に押してある。
これらの絵柄は　代々店に出入する
絵師や茶人たちの示唆によるもの。
亀屋伊織

い
ね
せ
ん
べ
い

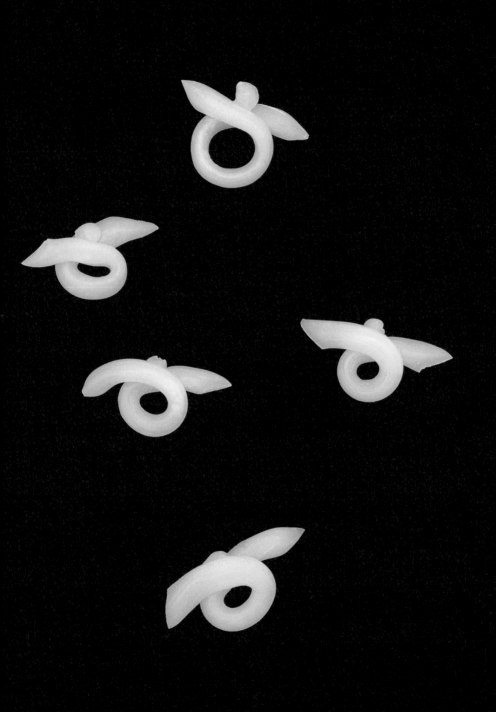

Straw Bag

Tawara, October
Autumn is the harvest season
in the rice producing country Japan.
The harvested grains are threshed and
packed into *tawara*, straw bags.
Thus *tawara* became a symbol of wealth.
Ōban and *koban*,
the large and small oval gold coins formerly
used in Japan are modeled
after a *tawara* filled with rice.
Kameyaiori

俵　十月
秋は米作国日本の収穫の季節。
穫れた米は脱穀して　俵に詰められる。
俵は富の表象　昔の金貨の大判・小判も
新米のぎっしり詰まった俵を象っている。
亀屋伊織

た
わ
ら

すずめ

雀　十月
稲が熟する頃　田んぼに来るスズメを
稲雀と言い　追うと同時に親しんでも来た。
黄色の有平糖をくるりとねじっただけの雀は
亀屋伊織の干菓子の中でも傑作の一つ。
亀屋伊織

Suzume, October
Suzume, the sparrows,
visiting the fields to peck at the ripe grains
of rice are called *inasuzume,* rice sparrows.
We try to scare them away and feel affection
for them at the same time. This is one of the
masterpieces among Kameya Iori's *higashi,*
dried confections. By simply twisting
the yellow *aruheitō,* toffee, a sparrow is suggested.
Kameyaiori

Sparrow

はつかり

初雁　十月
ガンはカリ　またはカリガネと言い
十月はじめ　北方から来る秋の渡り鳥。
とくに最初に見るものを初雁と言い
古来、和歌や俳諧にうたわれて来た。
亀屋伊織

Hatsukari, October
Gan, wild goose, is referred to as *kari* or *karigane*,
voice of the wild geese.
The migrating birds from the
north begin arriving in early October.
The first flock of geese arriving is called *hatsukari*,
the first wild geese, and has been the subject
of *waka* and *haikai* poetry since ancient times.
Kameyaiori

The First Wild Geese

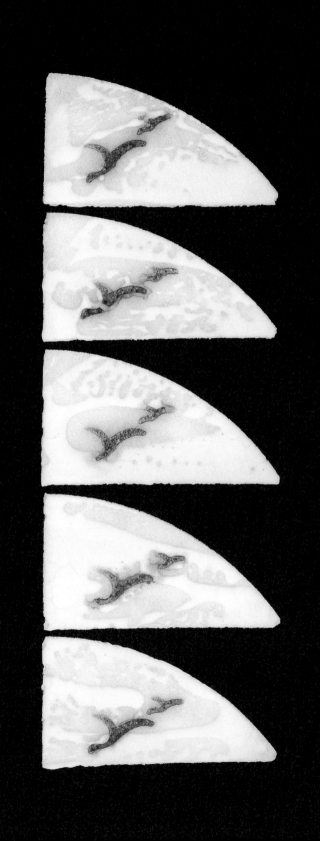

なるこ

鳴子　十月
熟した稲を食べに来る鳥たちを追う鳥威し
その代表が鳴子で　引板ともいう。
絵馬型の板に竹管が掛けつらねてあり
縄を引くと管が鳴って鳥を威すのだ。
亀屋伊織

Naruko,　October
Among bird rattles which are used to scare
away the birds coming to peck at the ripe grains of rice,
a typical one is the *naruko*, clapper,
which is also called *hita*, pulling board.
Several bamboo pipes are attached to a board
in the shape of an *ema,* a votive tablet with a picture
of a horse seen at shrines.
It makes a loud rattling sound when the rope
connecting to the *naruko* is pulled,
thus frightening the birds.
Kameyaiori

Bird Rattle

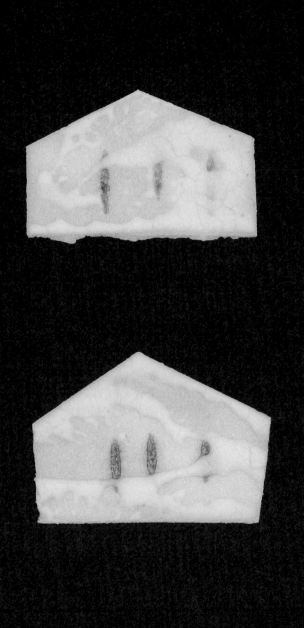

あきびより

秋日和　九月
秋の快晴の日は空気が澄みわたり
一年じゅうでいちばん心地よいもの。
野に咲く一輪のキキョウの姿に
秋日和を収斂させた。
とらや

Akibiyori, September
On a fine day in autumn the air is perfectly clear.
This is the most refreshing time of the year.
A lovely autumn day is distilled in the figure of *kikyō*,
a Japanese bellflower.
Toraya

A Lovely Autumn Day

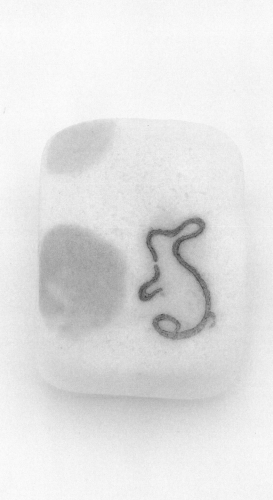

たつたのさと

竜田の里　九月
あらし吹く三室の山のもみぢばは
龍田の川のにしきなりけり－
能因法師の歌にいう三室山も龍田川も
龍田の里を彩る紅葉の名どころだ。
とらや

Tatsuta no sato,　September
The colored leaves
Of Mount *Mimuro*
Where the storm was blowing,
Have become the brocade
Of the River Tatsuta.
Both Mount Mimuro and the River Tatsuta,
mentioned in this poem composed
by Buddhist priest Nō in,
are places near the village of Tatsuta
famous for colored leaves.
Toraya

Village in Tatsuta

げっかのうたげ

月下の宴　九月
仲秋の名月（陰暦八月十五夜）とともに
後の月（同九月十三夜）を賞さなければ、
月を愛でたことにならないとか。
月を眺めるウサギを焼きつけた薯蕷饅頭。
とらや

Gekka no utage, September
A proper moon viewing includes
appreciating both *Chūshū no Meigetu,*
the full moon on fifteenth day
of the Eighth Month in the Chinese lunar calendar,
and *Nochi no Tsuki,* the moon two days
before the full moon on the thirteenth day
of the Ninth Month in the Chinese lunar calendar, respectively.
A brand mark of a rabbit looking up at the moon
is on the top of a *jōyomanjū,*
a steamed yam bun with bean jam inside.
Toraya

Banquet under the Moon

Rabbit Cake

Usagiman, September
The symbolic animals of the moon we find in *saijiki*,
seasonal almanacs, are the Rabbit in the moon,
the Rat in the moon, and the Frog in the moon. . .
However, only the Rabbit became a confection.
It would surely be unappetizing
to have Rat Cakes or Frog Cakes.
Toraya

兎饅　九月
歳時記に出てくる月の象徴動物は
月のウサギ、月のネズミ、月のカエル・・・・
しかし、お菓子になれるのはウサギだけ。
ネズミ饅頭、カエル饅頭ではやはり困る。
とらや

うさぎまん

き
く
の
か

菊の香　九月
秋のキクは春のウメとともに
古代中国から舶来した花。
その高貴な香りは不老長寿をもたらすものと
大切にされて　今日に至っている。
とらや

Kiku no ka, September
Both autumn's *kiku*,
chrysanthemum, and spring's *ume*,
plum tree, were brought from ancient China.
The chrysanthemum's noble fragrance,
which is said to invite eternal life and youth,
has been venerated ever since.
Toraya

Fragrance of Chrysanthemum

ちよみぐさ

千代見草　九月
千代見草はキクの異名の一つ
周の穆王（ぼくおう）の侍童は南陽郡麗県山（れきけんざん）に流されたが
その地で菊の露を飲み　不老不死になったという。
能「菊慈童」　またの名「枕慈童」で知られる。
とらや

Chiyomigusa, September
Chiyomigusa is another name for *kiku*,
chrysanthemum.
A legend tells of a boy in service to King Boku of
Chou who was exiled to Mount Rekiken in Nanyōgun.
There the boy drank from the leaf of a chrysanthemum
a dewdrop which was reflecting
a sutra and thus became immortal.
The story became the basis for a Noh play,
"*Kikujidō*", "*Crysanthemum* Boy"; also called as
"*Makurajidō*", "Pillow Boy".
Toraya

Seeing A Thousand Years Grass

Chestnut Fawn Cake

Kuri kanoko, September

The *kuri,* chestnuts, ripen and their first burs
begin to fall from trees around the time of *Nochi no Tsuki,*
the thirteenth-day moon in the Ninth Month
in the Chinese lunar calendar.
The newly harvested chestnuts are honeyed
and then used to cover the surface of the bean jam cake.
The cake reminds us of the white spots on a fawn's back.

Toraya

栗鹿の子　九月

陰暦九月十三日　後の月の頃は

ちょうどクリが実り　はじめて落ちる頃。

その年穫れた栗を蜜漬けして　餡玉に着せ

仔鹿の背の白い斑紋に見立てた。

とらや

くりかのこ

はつせのにしき

初瀬の錦　九月
王朝時代の女性たちの信仰を集め
女流日記にもしばしば登場する長谷寺。
長谷寺のある初瀬もまた紅葉の名どころ
重なる紅葉で錦秋を表現した。
とらや

Hatsuse no Nishiki, September
Hase Temple, which inspired faith
from many women in the Monarchic Age,
appears often in the court ladies' diaries.
Hatsuse, where the temple is located,
is also a viewing spot for tinted leaves.
The design of one tinted leaf laid
on another typifies *kinshū*,
the season for colored leaves.
Toraya

Brocade in Hatsuse

Four Seasons of Mount Fuji   Autumn

Shiki no fuji Aki, September
The twenty-sixth day of the Seventh Month
in the Chinese lunar calendar was the day Mount Fuji
was closed to climbers for the season.
The rain around this time is called
Mount Fuji's *oyamaarai,* mountain wash.
Of course, it clears up after that and the *akanezora,*
crimson sunset sky,
makes the whole mountain as well
as the morning it self stand out.
Toraya

四季の富士　秋　九月
陰暦七月二十六日は富士閉山の日－
この頃降る雨を富士の御山洗という。
もちろん　その後は晴れわたり
いちめんの茜空が朝ごと山容を際立たせる。
とらや

し
き
の
ふ
じ

あ
き

ちよのきく

千代の菊　十月
王朝時代の宮中では　キクに綿を置き
置綿（おきわた）に結ぶ露を朝採って　献上し
天皇の長寿を願ったという。
渦巻模様が悠久の時を表わす。
とらや

Chiyo no kiku, October
In the Imperial Court in the Monarchic Age,
a piece of silk called *okiwata* was placed
over a chrysanthemum flower to gather the morning dew.
The dew was offered to the Emperor as a wish
for his longevity.
The whirl shape represents time moving off into eternity.
Toraya

A Thousand Years' Chrysanthemum

むらさきの

紫野　十月
あかね　　むらさきの　　　しめの
茜さす紫野行き標野行き
のもり
野守は見ずや君が袖振る
おおあまのみこ　ぬかたのおおきみ
大海人皇子と額田王の恋で知られる紫野

ムラサキグサの名は根の紫色から来ている。

とらや

Murasakino, October
Shining brightly,
The field of madder you are riding,
The enclosed field you are crossing.
Could the gamekeeper have seen you
Waving your sleeve at me?
Murasakino of Kyoto, the field of madder,
is famous for the love between
Ōamanomiko Crown Prince Ōama,
and Nukatanōkimi, Lady Nukata.
The name *murasakigusa*, purple grass,
came from the madder's purple colored root.
Toraya

The Field of Madder

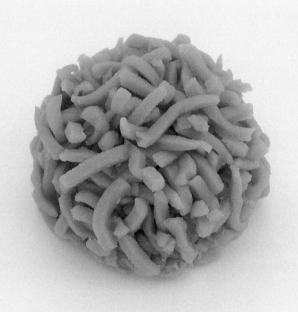

The First Wild Geese

Hatsukari, October
From terms such as, *kari no retsu*,
a line of flying geese, and *kari no sao*,
a pole of flying geese,
we are aware of the bird's habit
of flying in a strict row.
By pressing a brand of three wild geese on a *jōyomanjū*,
the confection represents the birds flying
in the vanguard like *monomi*, scouts.

Toraya

初雁　十月
雁の列　雁の棹という形容のとおり
ガンは整然と列を組んで渡ることで知られているが、
これは薯蕷饅頭に三羽だけの焼印を押すことで
斥候のように先頭を行く雁を表わした。

とらや

はつかり

まろにえ

マロニエ　十月
マロニエはトチノキ科の落葉高木。
フランスやイタリアの街路樹で知られる。
パリ店出店10周年を記念して作られた
新時代にふさわしい新感覚の菓子。
とらや

Maronie, October
Maronie, horse chestnut, belongs to *tochinokika*,
the Horse chestnut family.
It is a tall deciduous tree.
It is also known as a tree seen along streets
in France and Italy.
This confection was made to celebrate
the tenth anniversary of the opening
of the Paris branch of Toraya.
A confection that matches the new sensibility of a new age.
Toraya

Horse Chestnut

こねりがき

木練柿　十月
木になったままで甘くなったカキを
木煉柿、または単に木煉、煉柿ともいう。
狂言「合柿」に出てくる木煉はこれで
完熟前摘果の現在は　なかなかお目にかかれない。
とらや

Konerigaki,　October
Kaki, a persimmon fruit,
that ripened on the tree is called *konerigaki*,
tree-ripened persimmon, or simply *koneri*, or *nerigaki*.
It is the same *koneri* as the one appearing
in the *Kyōgen* farce, "*Awasegaki*", "Matching Persimmons".
In our time, the fruits are harvested
before they ripen on the trees so we seldom encounter
this tree-ripened persimmon.
Toraya

Tree-Ripened Persimmon 　　　346

Chrysanthemum on the Mountain Path

Yamaji no kiku, October
A fragrant *kiku*, chrysanthemum,
one unexpectedly encounters
while walking along the mountain path.
To the white chrysanthemum shaped *jōyomanjū*,
a leaf made of *yōkan*, jellied bean paste, is added.
Toraya

山路の菊　十月
秋の山路を歩いていて　思いがけなく
見いだした　香り高い一輪のキク。
白い菊花を象った薯蕷饅頭に
羊羹製の一枚の葉を添えた。
とらや

やまじのきく

Master Grass

Arujigusa, October

Arujigusa, the master grass,
is one of the refined names of *kiku,* chrysanthemum.
It is an elegant name used in *waka* or *tanka* poetry,
meaning *kusa no aruji,* the master of the grasses.
The name might be suggesting that *kiku* rules
the entire grass kingdom.

Toraya

主草　十月
主草とは菊の美称の一つ　草の主を
歌ことば的に言い換えた雅びやかな表現。
草花の王者として　すべての草花を
統べているというほどの意味だろう。
とらや

あるじぐさ

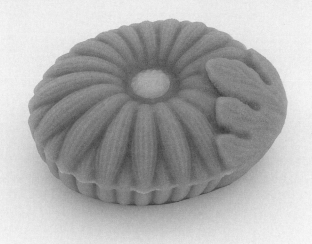

落雁

Descending Geese

The roots of *rakugan* can be traced back to the late
Jōmon Period. It is an *oshigashi*, pressed confection,
made by pressing the *okoshiganeko*,
powder of steamed and dried glutinous rice and chestnuts,
in a wooden mould. Beginning in the Muromachi Period,
the appearance of *rakugan* with black sesame seeds sprinkled
over the white paste was said to resemble the
"*Heisarakugan*", "Wild geese descending in the desert"
which is found in a famous series
of eight scenic places depicted in Chinese paintings,
called "Shōshōhakkei".
In the course of time,
"*Heisa*" was forgotten and it became a simple "*Rakugan*".
A variety of wooden moulds and different choices
of color have added a considerable number of sweets
to the repertoire of *wagashi*,
Japanese confectionery.

落雁
ルーツは縄文後期まで辿れるという
おこし種粉を木型に入れて押す押菓子。
室町の頃　白生地に黒胡麻を振ったさまが
沙上に群雁が落ちるのに似ていると、
漢画題「瀟湘八景」の「平沙落雁」を当てた。
いつか平沙は忘れられて　ただの落雁。
木型により　色と形のヴァリアント豊富、
和菓子の一レパートリーを占める。

らくがん

は␤な␤の␤え␤ん Flower Viewing Party

はるのかざし

Spring Flower on One's Cap

はなみぐるま

Cherry Blossom Viewing Cart

はるのひかり

Spring Light

きりつぼ Paulownia Court

<ruby>浄白<rt>じやうはく</rt></ruby>の<ruby>懐紙<rt>くわいし</rt></ruby>にのりたる

Placed on a chaste paper napkin,

<ruby>薄桃<rt>うすもも</rt></ruby>いろの<ruby>菓子<rt>くわし</rt></ruby>はゆかしや

How graceful is the pale pink confection.

しろがねの<ruby>楊枝<rt>やうじ</rt></ruby>もて切られ

Cut with a silver stylet,

をみなごの<ruby>朱唇<rt>しゆしん</rt></ruby>へとはこばるゝ

Then carried to the maiden's crimson lips,

そのたまゆらの<ruby>距離<rt>きより</rt></ruby>うつくしや

How beautiful the twinkle's distance.

失名氏　　Anonymous

もう一つの季節感　和菓子序説

　現在私達が何気なく使っている菓子という二字の古い訓みは「くだもの」だった。くだものは、木のものの訛り、木にみのる果実こそがわが国の菓子の原型だった。定時の質素な食事の直後やはざまに、木から直接採った果実、あるいはそれらを干したものを食べて、口腹の愉しみとしたのである。

　平安初期、醍醐天皇の延喜年間といえば、わが国最初の勅撰和歌集『古今和歌集』の完成した時代だが、同じ延喜年間の宮廷でまとめられた重要な書物がある。その書物の名は『延喜式』、その名のとおり、延喜年間当時の朝廷の年中儀式や制度の実施細則を漢文で記したものだ。その中の天皇の食事関係の決まりをまとめた「大膳」の部に「諸国貢進菓子」の項がある。当時の朝廷が支配した各地方から貢ぎものとして進らせる菓子の種類と量を示したものだ。

　国名は、山城、大和、河内、摂津、和泉、伊賀、伊勢、遠江、駿河、伊豆、甲斐、相模、近江、出羽、越前、加賀、能登、越中、越後、丹波、但馬、因幡、出雲、播磨、美作、備前、備中、紀伊、阿波、太宰府（筑紫）の三十一箇国。近国

Another measure of the seasons

—— An Introduction to Japanese Confections ——

The ancient reading for the two Chinese characters now used for *kashi* or confection was *kudamono*, fruit and nuts. *Kudamono* came from *kinomono*, things from trees. The prototype of our country's confectionery was fruits and nuts. Fruits fresh from trees or dried were eaten between humble meals or after them as a treat.

Emperor Daigo's Engi Era of the early Heian Period (8th century–12th century C.E.) was known for the accomplishment of the first national anthology of *waka* poetry, *Kokinwakashū*. Another important book, *Engishiki*, which recorded the detailed administration of the annual events and institutions of the Imperial Court in the Chinese language, was also compiled during the same Era. In '*Taizen*', its chapter on the Emperor's diet, there is a section on the confections presented to the Court by the provinces. It lists both the types and amounts of confections the provinces within the Empire were presenting to the Emperor.

There were thirty-one provinces listed: Yamashiro, Yamato, Kawachi, Settsu, Izumi, Iga, Ise, Tōtōmi, Suruga, Izu, Kai, Sagami, Ōmi, Dewa, Echizen, Kaga, Noto, Etchū, Echigo, Tanba,Tajima, Inaba, Izumo, Harima, Misaku, Bizen, Bitchū, Kii, Awa, Dazaifu, and Tsukushi. Things such as mube (Stauntonia vine), *akebi* (akebia), *ichigo* (strawberry), *yamamomo* (myrica), *kuri*

ではムベ、アケビ、イチゴ、ヤマモモ、クリ、シイなど、コウジ（＝ミカン）、ナシ、変わったところではレンコンもある。遠国で目立つのは甘葛煎〔あまずらせん〕、これは現在言うところのアマチャヅルの茎を冬期切り、切断面から滴下する液を集めて濃縮し、甘味料としたもので、これを甕などの容器に入れて保存したらしい。

　甘葛煎の貢進量はかなり多く、この時期すでに古来の菓子＝くだもののほかに、甘味料を要する新しい菓子が海外から到来していたことを示している。それら新しい菓子は海外から来たという意味で唐菓子と呼ばれた。この時代よりやや遅れて出た一種の百科事典『倭名類聚抄』には「八種唐菓子〔やくさのからくだもの〕」として、梅枝〔ばいし〕、桃枝〔とうし〕、餲餬〔かっこ〕、桂心〔けいしん〕、粘臍〔てんせい〕、䉏䭔〔ひちら〕、槌子〔ついし〕、団喜〔だんき〕を挙げている。唐果物の多くは米粉、麦粉に甘葛を加えて練り固めたものを、茹〔ゆ〕でて、のち油で揚げたようだ。八種のほかにも十種以上の名が知られ、後のうどんやおこし、せんべいの元になったものもある。

　本来の菓子＝くだものに新来の菓子が加わり、からくだものと呼ばれるようになると、本来の菓子はきくだものと呼ばれるようになる。本来木のものの転訛であるくだものにまた木をつけるのだから畳語ということになるが、唐くだものと

(chestnut), *shii* (chinquapin), *kōji* or *mikan* (mandarin orange), *nashi* (pear), and *renkon* (lotus root) were reported to have been sent from nearby provinces. From more distant provinces, the most notable product was a natural sweetener, *amazurasen*, condensed syrup made from *amachazuru*, a species of hydrangea. It was thought to have been collected during winter by gathering the sap from the cut stems, which was then condensed and stored in a jar.

The amount of *amazursen* presented was quite large, which suggests that in addition to the original fruits and nuts, a new kind of confectionery made with added sweetener had already been introduced from abroad. Since they came from abroad, those new confections were called *kara-kudamono*, Tang confectionery. An encyclopedia, *Wamyōruijōshō*, published some time later contains *yagusa no kara-kudamono*, eight kinds of Tang confectioneries, called *baishi, tōshi, kakko, keishin, tensei, hichira, tsuishi,* and *danki.* Most were made of rice or wheat flour combined with *amazurasen.* They were kneaded and boiled, then deep fried in oil. More than ten additional confections were known besides these eight. Some were believed to have become prototypes for noodles, rice cakes, and rice crackers.

When the newly imported confections were introduced and named *kara-kudamono*, people started calling the regular *kudamono* by the name of *ki-kudamono*, meaning either tree-fruits or fresh-fruits. Also they started to use the term *tsukuri-kudamono*, crafted-confectionery,

差別化するために木を付けたのだろう。生くだものという解釈もありうる。また、木くだものに対して、唐くだものを作りくだものというようにもなったが、木に実った自然の菓子に対して人工の菓子をいうのだから、こちらの方が論理に適っている。

　いずれにしても、唐菓子の詳細はわからない。これを司っていたのは宮中大膳職主菓餅だが、公家社会が武家社会になって朝廷が衰退し朝廷機構が名ばかりのものになったことが大きな原因だろう。代わって新しい唐菓物・作りくだものの中心となったのは、武家に支持された新来の仏教、禅宗の寺院だった。そこに伝えられた喫茶・点心の習慣は、定時の食事以外に茶とともに小さな間食をするという日本人の風習を産んだ。

　点心の範囲は広く、粥や汁・麺類まで含むが、のちに大きな影響を与えたものに、羹類、饅頭類がある。中国の民間では本来そのどちらにも肉を入れたが、禅院ではこれを嫌い肉の代わりに豆類を用いた。字の意味としては羊の羹をいうのはずの羊羹が小豆から成り、かの地では豚肉などの入った饅頭がわが国で豆餡なのも、禅院の製法が天武天皇の禁令以来肉類忌避のわが国の嗜好に合って定着したということだろう。これらの菓子は以

for *kara-kudamono*. This sounds natural when we consider how they were made, in contrast to regular *kudamono*, which were simply gathered from trees.

We do not know much about *kara-kudamono*. This lack of information may have been caused by the shift of power from the aristocrats to the warriors, which had weakened the functioning of offices in the Imperial Court, including the Imperial Confectionery Department. The center for *kara-kudamono* shifted from the Court to the temples of the newly introduced Zen Buddhist sect, which was supported by the warrior class. From their habit of drinking tea and eating *tenshin*, Buddhist monk's snack, a new practice of taking a light snack with tea between meals was introduced into Japanese life.

The varieties of *tenshin* are numerous, including rice porridge, soup, and noodles. The most influential ones were *atsumono*, a thick vegetable and meat soup served hot, and *manjū*, steamed buns with vegetables and meat inside. In China both originally contained meat, but in Zen temples where meat was not normally eaten, the meat was replaced with beans. One kind of *tenshin* is *yōkan* which literally means mutton soup, but it is made with bean jam made from adzuki beans. The steamed buns originally contained meat in China, but in our country the meat was replaced by bean jam. From these facts we know that the vegetarian style brought by Zen monks conformed to the situation in our country where the ban on eating meat had been enforced by the Emperor

後独自の発達を遂げる。これが木くだものでもない、唐くだものでもない、和菓子である。

　和菓子の主流は、茶の湯の席で喫茶の前に食べるいわゆる茶席菓子である。しかし、茶の湯の大成者、千利休の頃の茶席菓子はまだ寥々たるものだった。干柿や焼栗、せいぜいが麦粉を薄く溶いて焼いたふの焼き程度だった。初期の茶席菓子に限っていえば、木くだものが主流だったのである。これは茶の湯のかたちが応仁の乱から戦国時代にかけてのいわゆる乱世にしだいに固まって行ったことを考えれば当然であろう。優雅、さらには華麗な菓子を作る余裕など、戦乱のあいまの茶席にあったろうはずはない。

　利休の孫、宗旦から出た三千家（表千家、裏千家、武者小路千家）、また宗旦四天王に代表される弟子家筋の発展とともに、茶席菓子はレパートリーを拡げ、色・形を極めて行った。側面からそれを支えたのは徳川将軍三百年の泰平の治世だ。レパートリーの拡大は季節感の細分化ともいえる。茶の湯は年間を通しておこなわれるものだが、初釜、風炉、朝茶、口切、炉開、夜咄などの変化はあるものの、飲みものとしての茶自体は一律で変化に乏しい。季節感に乏しい茶に代わって、これを代行するのが発展した茶席菓

Tenmu since the seventh century. From this time on, the Japanese confectionery followed an independent path of development. Thus *wagashi*, Japanese confectionery, which is neither *ki-kudamono* nor *kara-kudamono* was born.

The most prominent confection among the *wagashi* is *chasekigashi*, tea-room confection, eaten at tea ceremony before sipping a bowl of tea. But at the time of the founder of tea ceremony, Sen no Rikyū, the confectionery served was still a plain natural product such as dried persimmons, roasted chestnuts, or at most thin crepes made of wheat flour.

Thus if we restrict our comments to the early period of the development of *chasekigashi*, we could say that *ki-kudamono* was still the mainstream. This is only natural when we consider that the formative period of the art of tea ceremony took place during the turbulent times from the civil war of the Ōnin Era to the Age of Civil Wars. There would have been little opportunity to seek elegance and refinement in the confections served at the tea ceremonies held between battles.

The *chasekigashi* broadened its repertoire, refining its shape and color, as the three Sen clans, Omote Senke, Ura Senke, and Mushakōji Senke, which descended from Sōtan, a grandson of Rikyū, and the families of his disciples who were known as "the Big Four" prospered. The three hundred years of peace under the Tokugawa regime made this growth possible. This expansion of repertoire allowed a subdivision of the confections

子だった。各季各月どんな菓子があるか、菓子暦で見てみよう。茶の暦は十一月から始まるから、それに従おう。

十一月　龍田餅（たつたもち）　吹き寄せ（ふきよせ）
　　　　山路の錦（やまじにしき）

十二月　袴腰餅（はかまごしもち）　雪輪（ゆきわ）　冬籠（ふゆごもり）

一月　　菱葩餅（ひしはなびらもち）　千代結（ちよむすび）　春隣（はるどなり）

二月　　梅衣（うめごろも）　狐面（きつねめん）　椿餅（つばきもち）

三月　　若草（わかくさ）　貝尽くし（かいづくし）　菜種の里（なたねのさと）

四月　　花筏（はないかだ）　蝶々（ちょうちょう）　春の夢（はるのゆめ）

五月　　粽（ちまき）　葵（あおい）　岩根のつつじ（いわね）

六月　　青梅（あおうめ）　蛍煎餅（ほたるせんべい）　水のほとり（みず）

七月　　天の川（あまのがわ）　糸巻（いとまき）　青梨（あおなし）

八月　　葉月（はづき）　観世水（かんぜすい）　夕涼み（ゆうすず）

九月　　萩の餅（はぎのもち）　枝豆（えだまめ）　月下の宴（げっかのうたげ）

十月　　亥の子餅（いのこもち）　初雁（はつかり）　山路の菊（やまじのきく）

　現行の茶席菓子は、花、葉、果実を象（かたど）るなど、植物のかたちが多い。その点ではわが国原初の菓子＝木くだものが作りくだものの方法を使って復活したかのようだが、それだけではなく、天象もあれば行事もある。それにしてもなんといううつくしい呼び名づくめだろう。いや、呼び名だけではない。その色と形の美しさ、ほのかな甘さと香り高さ、和菓子の暦は実際の暦とはもう一つ別の暦。菓子が菓子であることを超えて体系化され、文化であり、教養でさえある国は、日本以外にはあるまい。
　　　　　　　　　　　　　　　　高橋睦郎

based on a sense of the seasons. Tea ceremony is performed throughout the year on occasions like *hatsugama*, the first tea ceremony of the year, *furo*, summer tea ceremony, *asacha*, tea ceremony on a summer morning, *kuchikiri*, opening of the first tea container of the year in November, *robiraki*, opening of the sunken hearth, and *yobanashi*, tea ceremony held on a winter evening. The tea itself as a beverage remains the same throughout the year, lacking variation. Since it is thus not possible for the tea to evoke a seasonal feeling, the characteristics of the *chasekigashi* were developed to give a sense of the seasons.

I would like to follow the tea ceremony calendar and take a look at the seasonal and monthly specialties of the tea ceremony sweets beginning with November when the New Year begins.

November: *Tatsutamochi,* Tatsuta Cake, *Fukiyose,* Wind-driven Leaves, *Yamaji no nishiki,* Brocade of the Mountain Path

December: *Hakamagoshimochi,* Pleated Skirt Cake, *Yukiwa,* Snow Ring, *Fuyugomori,* Winter Hibernation

January: *Hishihanabiramochi,* Flower Petal Cake, *Chiyomusubi,* Chiyo Knot, *Harudonari,* Spring in the Neighborhood

February: *Umegoromo,* Plum Blossom Robe, *Kitsunemen,* Fox Mask, *Tsubakimochi,* Camellia Cake

March: Wakakusa, Young Grass, Kaizukushi, Shellfish Collection, *Natane no sato,* Village of Rape Flowers

April: *Hanaikada,* Cherry Petal Raft, *Chocho,* Butterfly, *Haru no yume,* Spring Dream

May: *Chimaki*, Bamboo Grass Leaf Wrap, *Aoi*, Mallow, *Iwane no tsutsuji*, Azalea at the Foot of a Rock

June: *Aoume*, Green Plum, *Hotaru senbei*, Firefly Rice Crackers, *Mizu no hotori*, The Water's Edge

July: *Ama no gawa*, The Milky Way, *Itomaki*, Spool, *Aonashi*, Green

August: *Hazuki*, Leaf Month, *Kanzesui*, Whirlpool, *PearYusuzumi*, Evening Cool

September: *Hagi no mochi*, Japanese Bush Clover Cake, *Edamame*, Green Soybean, *Gekka no Utage*, Banquet under the Moon

October: *Inoko mochi*, Boar Day Cake, *Hatsukari*, The First Wild Geese, *Yamaji no kiku*, Chrysanthemum on the Mountain Path

Many current *chasekigashi* are modeled after plants, taking the shapes of flowers, leaves, and fruits. It is as if the original sweets of this country, *ki-kudamono*, fruits, are revived by means of *tsukuri-kudamono*, artificial confectionery. But there are other kinds, too. There are confections that are modeled after astronomical phenomenon and yearly events as well. And what a beautiful name each one of them is given! Not only the names, but also the beauty of their shapes and colors, their delicate sweetness and fragrance! In addition to the ordinary calendar, *wagashi* can be said to have become another Japanese calendar. There may not be another country besides Japan where the confectionery has gone beyond simply being confectionery, where it has been systematized to such extent that it has even become an element of culture, a sophistication.   Mutsuo Takahashi

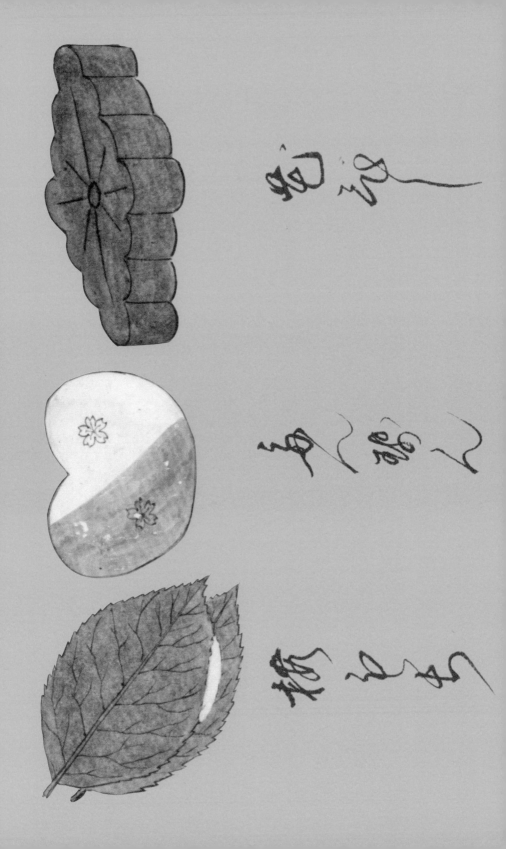

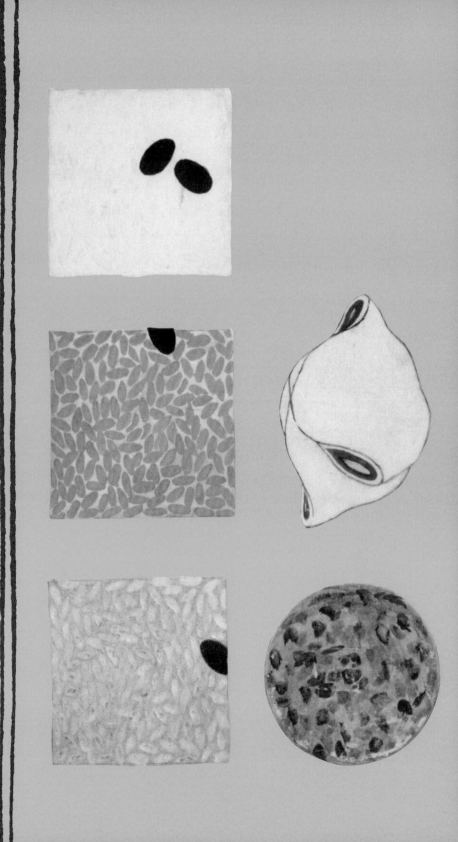

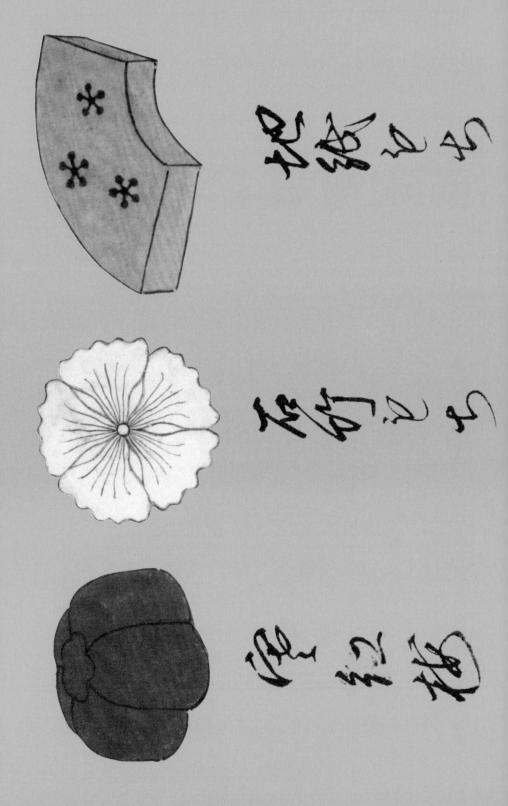

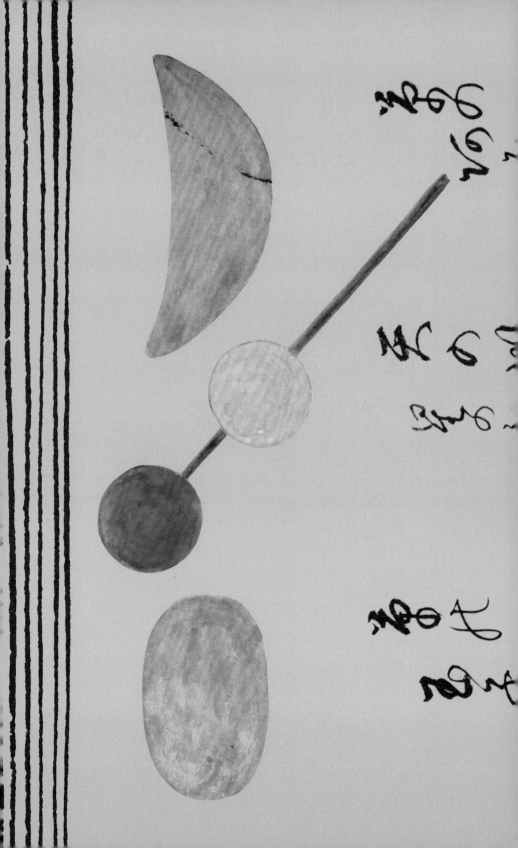

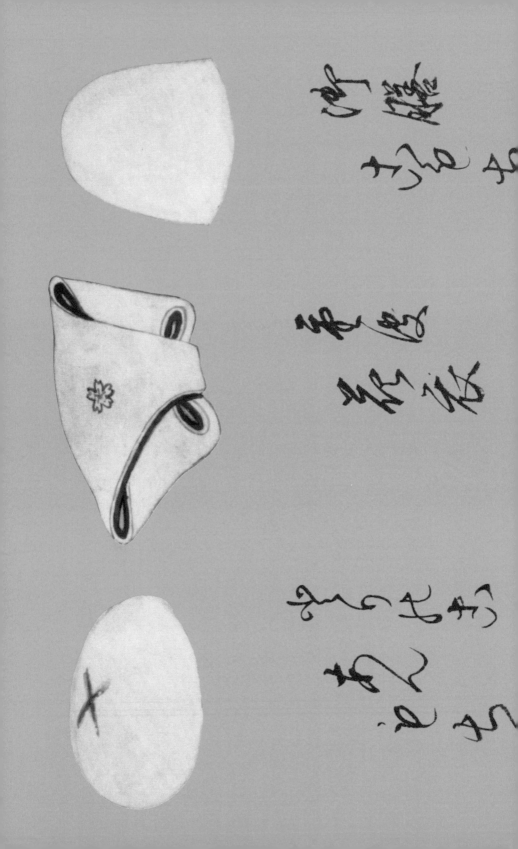

和
の

WAGASHI

菓
子

Co-operation

Kawabata Dōki
2-12, Shimogamo Minamino Nogamichō, Sakyō-ku, Kyōto 606-0817

Kameya Iori
Nijyōdori Shinmachi Higashi, Nakakyō-ku, Kyōto 604-0026

Toraya
4-9-22, Akasaka, Minato-ku, Tokyo 107-8401

7、10-11、63、66-67、111、114-117、175、178-179、295、298-299
from "Shaseichō, A Sketch Book" of Ōkyo Maruyama
(stored in Tokyo National Museum)

235、238-239
from "Sōka Shasei Zukan, Flowers Sketch Illustrated Book"
of Tanyu Kanō (stored in Tokyo National Museum)

377-382
from "Kawabata Dōki Wagashi Mihoncho, Kawabata Dōki
Confection Sample Book" (stored in Kawabata Dōki)

高岡一弥（たかおかかずや）　1945年、京都府生まれ。アートディレクター。主な著書に『千年』（毎日新聞社）、『野菜から見た肉』（パルコ出版）、『春・観る』（時事通信社）、『女性とエイズ』『Quality of Life』（日本財団）、『katachi』（ピエ・ブックス）、雑誌『活人』少女光線、日本未少年（毎日新聞社）。『彼方へ』『東京 LIVING WITH AIDS & HIV』等、展覧会イベントを主催。日宣美展特選、日本グラフィックデザイン展金賞、講談社出版文化賞受賞、他。

高橋睦郎（たかはしむつお）　1937年、北九州八幡生まれ。少年時代から詩、俳句、短歌、その他あらゆる詩形を試作し、現在に至る。二十二冊の詩集のほか、句集、歌集、小説集、評論集…など著書多数。また、演劇やオペラの台本、新作能、新作狂言など、舞台に関わり、国内外での自作詩朗読にも力をそそぐ。詩集『兎の庭』で高見順賞、句歌集『稽古飲食』で読売文学賞、台本修辞『王女メディア』でグローバル国際交流基金山本健吉賞…など受賞多数。2000年度紫綬褒章受章。文学、ことに日本文学の発生および歴史に関心深く、『読みなおし日本文学史──歌の漂泊』『十二夜──古典文学に親しむための』。俳句関係では『私自身のための俳句入門』『百人一句』などの著書がある。

与田弘志（よだひろし）　1942年、東京都生まれ。1961年ロンドンに移住し、ギルフォード スクール オヴ アート、ロンドン カレッジ オヴ プリンティング アンド グラフィクアーツ、デビッド・モンゴメリー スタジオで写真を学ぶ。1966年フリーランスのファッション写真家としてロンドンにて HIROSHI STUDIO を開き、活動。1972年からは、東京に本拠を移し、多くのファッション雑誌や企業広告に写真を発表。国内外で多くの個展を開催。ファッション・広告の第一線で活躍する写真家。講談社出版文化賞、東京アートディレクターズ・クラブ 最高賞、毎日広告賞最高賞受賞。写真集『TEA FOR TWO』（P-IKA PIKA）、『OBSESSION』、『HANAE MORI STYLE』（講談社インターナショナル）。

撮影協力

川端道喜（かわばたどうき）
〒606-0847 京都市左京区下鴨南野々神町2-12

亀屋伊織（かめやいおり）
〒604-0026 京都市中京区二条通新町東入ル

とらや
〒107-8401 東京都港区赤坂4-9-22

7、10-11、63、66-67、111、114-117、175、178-179、295、298-299
円山応挙「写生帖」東京国立博物館蔵

235、238-239
狩野探幽「草花写生図鑑」東京国立博物館蔵

4-5、377-382
川端道喜和菓子見本帳　川端道喜蔵

和の菓子

2003年9月17日 初版第1刷発行

アートディレクション 高岡一弥
選と文 高橋睦郎
写真 与田弘志

企画編集 高岡一弥
英訳 宮下惠美子 リー・ガーガ
デザイン 伊藤修一 淡海季史子 山崎恵
制作進行 小澤研太郎
制作進行協力 岸エミ香 山本智子
製版 稲川芳雄

発行者 三芳伸吾
発行所 ピエ・ブックス
〒170-0005 東京都豊島区南大塚2-32-4
編集 TEL: 03-5395-4820 FAX: 03-5395-4821
　　　E-mail: editor@piebooks.com
営業 TEL: 03-5395-4811 FAX: 03-5395-4812
　　　E-mail: sales@piebooks.com
http://www.piebooks.com

印刷・製本 大日本印刷株式会社
Book and cover design © 2003 Kazuya Takaoka
Selection and text © 2003 Mutsuo Takahashi
Photographs © 2003 Hiroshi Yoda
Translations © 2003 Emiko Miyashita & Lee Gurga
Published by PIE Books

ISBN 4-89444-288-4 C0072 Printed in Japan